# THE COHERENCE OF LIFE WITHOUT GOD BEFORE GOD

## The Problem of Earthly Desires in the Later Theology of Dietrich Bonhoeffer

Terrence Reynolds

UNIVERSITY
PRESS OF
AMERICA

Copyright © 1989 by

University Press of America,® Inc.

4720 Boston Way
Lanham, MD 20706

Library of Congress Cataloging-in-Publication Data

Reynolds, Terrence Paul, 1946–
The coherence of life without God before God : the problem of
earthly desires in the later theology of Dietrich Bonhoeffer / Terrence Reynolds.
p. cm.
Bibliography: p.
1. Bonhoeffer, Dietrich, 1906–1945—Contributions in doctrine of
earthly desires. 2. Spirituality—History of doctrines—20th
century. 3. Emotions—Religious aspects—Christianity—History of
doctrines—20th century. I. Title.
BV4490.R47     1988
233—dc 19     88–8489 CIP
ISBN 0–8191–7237–5 (alk. paper)

All University Press of America books are produced on acid-free paper.
The paper used in this publication meets the minimum requirements of American
National Standard for Information Sciences—Permanence of Paper for Printed Library
Materials, ANSI Z39.48–1984.     ∞

# TABLE OF CONTENTS

# PREFACE

This study was generated by a fascination with Dietrich Bonhoeffer which goes back many years. In recent months this interest has focused upon Bonhoeffer's later thought (1939-1945), and particularly upon his praise and encouragement of personal longings, and his call to Christian life "without God before God". Before 1939, Bonhoeffer was willing, at most, to tolerate and permit secular desires insofar as they assisted in carrying out God's preservative purposes for the fallen creation. But in the Letters and Papers from Prison, he unambiguously extols personal longings as valuable in themselves, and urges the Christian to feel his earthly desires to the fullest. He adds, suggestively, that the believer's love of God (cantus firmus) makes possible the relative independence of one's desires from God and His purposes, and somehow assists these longings to develop as powerfully as possible, wholly for themselves.

I've attempted to analyze this positive assessment of earthly desires in the Letters through an examination of the Ethics, which Bonhoeffer composed in the first draft fragments between 1939 and his arrest in the spring of 1943. I intend to show that a major shift in Bonhoeffer's thinking occurs after 1939 with respect to earthly life and human longings, and further, and perhaps more importantly, that these changes illustrate deeper shifts in his Christian anthropology and ethics. I believe that this provocative matter has been overlooked in the course of Bonhoeffer scholarship, and hope that my efforts will prompt a further study of the issues involved.

As Bonhoeffer realized, people and relationships are more important than anything else in life, and in that spirit I wish to thank several persons for their efforts and thoughtfulness on my behalf. Whatever positive contribution this study makes will be largely due to them; of course, I assume all responsibility for its shortcomings. John Godsey, of Wesley Theological Seminary, graciously took an interest in my proposal and found time in his crowded schedule to give the project a careful reading and commentary. His detailed suggestions were very helpful in refining my argumentation at several key points. Wendell Dietrich, of Brown University, also read the final draft, and offered a sensitive and discerning critique for which I am most grateful. Subtle errors in both tone and substance were reduced as a result.

I especially wish to acknowledge a large intellectual and personal debt to Giles Milhaven for his devotion to my work. As a colleague and friend, he studied my efforts, and offered numerous suggestions which greatly improved their quality. I cannot thank him enough for his commitment to me and to the project.

I want also to thank Shelly Milhaven for her patience and care in typing the final draft. Thanks are also in order to Marc Borg of Oregon State University, to Walter Conser of The University of North Carolina at Wilmington, and to Michael Levine of LaTrobe University, whose friendship, concern and encouragement have always meant much more than they realized. Finally, I offer an inadequate expression of thanks to my wife, Lyn, and to our three children. They are, indeed, most important in my life, and I dedicate this book to them as a small token of my affection.

# INTRODUCTION

In a letter from Tegel prison to Eberhard Bethge, dated May 20, 1944, Dietrich Bonhoeffer explained to his friend how the love of God somehow made it possible for earthly love to develop to its limits. He wrote as follows:

> What I mean is that God wants us to love him eternally with our whole hearts - not in such a way as to injure or weaken our earthly love, but to provide a kind of cantus firmus to which the other melodies of life provide the counterpoint. One of these contrapuntal themes (which have their own complete independence but are related to the cantus firmus) is earthly affection... Where the cantus firmus is clear and plain, the counterpoint can be developed to its limits. The two are 'undivided and yet distinct', in the words of the Chalcedonian Definition... I wanted to tell you to have a good, clear cantus firmus; that is the only way to a full and perfect sound, when the counterpoint has a firm support and can't come adrift or get out of tune, while remaining a distinct whole in its own right.[1]

This puzzling encouragement of earthly affection, or human love, in relative independence from Christ, absent from all of Bonhoeffer's work before 1939 and yet predominant in his work in prison, is the subject of our inquiry.

During his imprisonment, Dietrich Bonhoeffer experienced an intense, personal longing for the life he had known before his arrest and began, for the first time, to grapple explicitly with the question of earthly, secular desires in the life of the Christian. Henceforward, the expressions "purely secular", "human", "earthly", and "fallen" will be employed to suggest desires for other persons or for earthly goods, desires which seek the desired for its own sake. The expressions will, at the same time, refer to aspects of life discernible in themselves without their relationship to God being discerned. The relative independence of these desires from God and His purposes is what distinguishes them from desires mediated through Christ. His existential and theological struggle led Bonhoeffer in his Letters to encourage and urge believers unambiguously to desire other persons and the good things of the earth for their own sake, in relative independence from the purposes of God in Jesus Christ.

Prior to 1939, Bonhoeffer described purely secular longings as "dark desires" and "turbid urges" and placed them in bold relief against genuine love for God and neighbor, agape, as created in the heart of the Christian by the Holy Spirit.[2] Secular desires are encouraged nowhere in Bonhoeffer's writings before 1939. At times, he does urge Christians to love the earth and its good things, but it is always to be a love mediated in and through Jesus Christ. For example, in a lecture in November of 1932 on "Thy Kingdom Come! The Prayer of the Church for God's Kingdom on Earth", Bonhoeffer specifically urges the believer to participate in earthly life. As he says, "Whoever loves God ...loves him as Lord of the earth as it is; and whoever loves the earth loves it as God's earth. Whoever loves God's kingdom, loves it wholly as God's kingdom, but he also loves it as God's kingdom on earth."[3] But this passage does not encourage the Christian to love the earth for its own sake, but for the sake of the Lord to Whom it belongs. The endorsement and encouragement of human, earthly desires, therefore, particularly the secular longing of loved ones to be with one another, is unique to the Bonhoeffer corpus.

In addition, Bonhoeffer's encouragement of personal longings suggests important shifts in his Christian anthropology and ethics. We will argue that Bonhoeffer's praise of earthly desires in the Letters and his call to a life "without God before God" are a culmination of a positive reappraisal of fallen, natural life begun in Chapter IV of the Ethics and steadily developed until his death. His affirmation of the intrinsic value of earthly goods and personal longings led Bonhoeffer to encourage Christians to devote themselves to fallen life "as if there were no God", but to do so from the force of their faith. This conception of the Christian way of life and its relation to the ethical, discussed in detail in Chapter VII of the Ethics, is unique to moral philosophy and Christian thought. Bonhoeffer argues for a new perspective on both the Christian person and sanctification, and for a bold Christian worldliness in relative independence of Christ.

Nevertheless, this dramatic movement in Bonhoeffer's thought has gone unnoticed by scholars,[4] despite its centrality in the Letters and its broader implications. This present study was undertaken to give to this provocative issue the attention it merits, and to pose the subsequent questions it raises.

This issue may have been overlooked, in part, as a result of the uneven course of Bonhoeffer scholarship itself. This inquiry proceeds on the premise that the theology of Dietrich Bonhoeffer was seriously misunderstood and distorted during the 1950's and 1960's, particularly in America and the English-speaking world. In the years which followed the publication of the Letters and Papers from Prison in 1951, Bonhoeffer's letters were picked apart by those in search of a theme, a fragment or a phrase which would appear to align Bonhoeffer with their particular theological cause. In response to that injustice, more serious scholars of Bonhoeffer began the task of asserting the coherence of his thought, and sought to portray the continuity and sustained theological development which marks his work. However, as the pendulum rightly swung away from the misappropriation of the Letters and toward an appreciation of the consistent patterns in Bonhoeffer's overall theological enterprise, it may have swung too far and underplayed some of the radical novelty in his later thought. His preoccupation with secular desires is a case in point, for in his treatment of human longings he breaks ground previously untilled in his work.

In the mid and late 1960's Bonhoeffer's name was evoked as a champion of a Christianity secularized almost beyond recognition. His portrayal of the "world come of age" and his calls to "holy worldliness", "religionless Christianity", and to a life "as if there were no God" were pulled from the context of his prison letters as well as from the context of his earlier writings, and used as supporting motifs for radical assessments of Christian faith and life which were totally disharmonious with Bonhoeffer's own thought. His name became inappropriately linked, thereby, with movements and thought forms to which his theology had virtually no discernible connection.

This popularity was due, in part, to Bonhoeffer's martyrdom at the hands of the Nazi authorities and to the trenchant aphorisms which color his later work. But neither of these attractions proved helpful in illuminating the conceptual consistency of his work. The frustrating result was that Bonhoeffer became a kind of cult figure and no coherent patterns of his thought were permitted to emerge. Despite the evidence to the contrary, he was finally named as an advocate of the theological cul-de-sac which was the "death of God" movement.

Two brief examples should suffice to make the point. In 1965, William Bartley III, writing in The New York Review of Books interpreted Bonhoeffer as follows:

It becomes rather urgent for a person holding
a view like Bonhoeffer's - that there is literally no need for Christianity or for God in an
adult world - to explain what if anything does
distinguish a Christian from others, and why,
indeed, anyone should in such circumstances
remain a Christian. It is precisely at this
point that Bonhoeffer, who is rarely profound,
but usually clear, becomes as vague as any
continental theologian. The role of the
Christian is conceived now as a fundamentally
ethical one of total engagement in social and
personal life in full collaboration with like-
minded liberal secularists.[5]

Bartley's assessment is woefully lacking in familiarity with
Bonhoeffer's thought, for one could hardly read Bonhoeffer and
conclude that he sees no need for God in an adult world or that
Christian faith has become superfluous. Bartley may have been
overmatched by Bonhoeffer's subtlety, and concluded that what he
had overlooked did not exist. In some fairness to Bartley, however,
his evaluation was consistent with others who similarly focused
upon themes and phrases from the Letters and, without regard to
Bonhoeffer's earlier work, drew extreme conclusions.

Thomas Altizer, William Hamilton, Paul Van Buren, John
A.T. Robinson and others invoked Bonhoeffer as a catalyst for the
"death of God" theology of the 1960's.[6] They argued, with differing
emphases and with differing levels of reliance upon Bonhoeffer, that
God must be eliminated in order that human freedom, social justice,
and a new world might come into being. It was to be a world free of
sin and guilt, a world open to human possibility unshackled by the
notion of a Father God. In 1965, in a work entitled The Secularization of Christianity, E.L. Mascall yoked Bonhoeffer with several
thinkers whose theological foundations were not his own:

It has...been suggested that the extreme
secularist note which characterizes Tillich,
Bonhoeffer, and Bultmann, to say nothing of
Robinson himself, is the product of a violent
swing from one extreme position to the other,
from a position which is all about God and
grace to one which is all about man and
nature.[7]

Mascall's reading of Bonhoeffer, as we will see, is as one-sided as was Bartley's. Grace and the believer's love of God are crucial to all that Bonhoeffer has to say about secular life. Lost to Mascall and to others who readily associated him with the "death of God" movement is the fact that Bonhoeffer never spoke of the "death of God", and explicitly argued for an arcane discipline of devotion and prayer, for faith in the God Who rules all history, for love of God as the foundation of meaningful life, and, finally, for a dialectic of life without God, before God. Bonhoeffer unambiguously claims that only in faith can one live natural life to its fullest. In addition, Bonhoeffer expressed strong misgivings about both Tillich and Bultmann in his Letters, misgivings which Mascall neglected to note.[8]

These secular interpreters turned their spotlights upon the "without God" dimension of Bonhoeffer's call in the Letters to life "without God before God". John A.T. Robinson, for example, writes that Bonhoeffer urges Christians to outgrow the kind of faith "in which 'Daddy' is always there in the background".[9] But he fails to stress that God must always be present and that faith is absolutely necessary if one is to live "as if there were no God".

These "religionless Christianity", "secular theology" readings of Bonhoeffer do not sense the full dimension of our problem. For Bonhoeffer straightforwardly claims that Christ alone makes it possible for the believer to desire other persons to the fullest in relative independence of His person and purposes. Only a believing love of God (cantus firmus) enables the Christian to live the contrapuntal, worldly dimensions of his life to their limits "as if there were no God". Bonhoeffer's account of earthly desires does not raise the problem of God's death or elimination. Rather, it raises a constellation of questions surrounding the way in which the believer can be both profoundly related to Christ and yet relatively independent of Him in living the natural life. Omitting the presence of God from this dialectic destroys it.

The point of this too brief excursus is not that the secular, "death of God" movement offered nothing of merit; its impact upon the theological world argues to the contrary. But its use of Bonhoeffer, often admittedly as a springboard,[10] did serious damage to the appreciation of his larger theological enterprise, and made necessary a scholarly reassessment.

That re-assessment was aided by the appearance of a number of studies which pointed to thematic continuities in the Bonhoeffer literature. These works carefully scrutinized the Bonhoeffer corpus from beginning to end, aided considerably by the writing of Eberhard Bethge's authoritative biography of Bonhoeffer, which appeared in 1967. Studies emerged in French by Andre Dumas (1968), in German by Heinrich Ott (1966), and Ernst Feil (1971), and in English by John Godsey (1960), John Phillips (1967), Larry Rasmussen (1972), Clifford Green (1976), and James Patrick Kelley (1980) to name a few,[11] in which the authors argued that Bonhoeffer sustains certain theological concerns throughout his writings. While there was hardly unanimity with respect to the nature of the dominant motifs in Bonhoeffer's theology,[12] there was agreement that the radical turn attributed to Bonhoeffer in his prison years was unjustified, and that in all his work he develops one consistent, theological thought. James Patrick Kelley analyzes the shift in Bonhoeffer scholarship as follows:

> ...for some who had explored the Bonhoeffer
> corpus more extensively this early enthusiasm
> for Bonhoeffer appeared to be a perfect case
> for the classic caveat which identifies friend-
> ly endorsements as worse than inimical
> attacks. As more and more of Bonhoeffer's ex-
> tant writings became accessible, some amaz-
> ingly sustained and pervasive theological ef-
> forts began to be discerned in them. In place
> of Bonhoeffer, the author of sometimes enig-
> matic aphorisms, a new figure began to emerge
> whose theological work appeared to have more
> systematic coherence than had been thought...
> In fact his perduring effort to make sense of
> Christian faith in a particularly secularized
> epoch of Western history began to appear to
> merit an equally sustained and disciplined
> examination by any who shared his inter-
> ests.[13]

This commendable approach to the Bonhoeffer corpus, however, was not without problems of its own. For in seeking to establish the continuities in Bonhoeffer's thought, scholars have been less willing to acknowledge the discontinuities in the later writings. The issue which prompts this study represents a case in point. Scholars have agreed that Bonhoeffer writes of a dialectic in earthly life as early as 1929 in Barcelona[14] and subsequently affirms that dialectic throughout his work. But it has not been recognized that Bonhoeffer nowhere affirms the fallen, earthly pole of that dialectic for its own sake until after 1939. Only then does he specifically and explicitly encourage Christians to live fallen earthly life to the fullest, in some sense independently of Christ and His purposes.

These more responsible scholars, then, have tended to focus so steadily upon the conservative "before God" pole of the dialectic as to reduce considerably the startling originality of Bonhoeffer's position. They have failed to heed Bonhoeffer's own insistence that he is doing something new in Christian theology,[15] as well as his unambiguous urging of the Christian to seek the fallen earth and its good things for their own sake. Their inability to recognize the relative independence of the counterpoints, their Selbständigkeit to use Bonhoeffer's phrase, places too heavy a Christological interpretation of Bonhoeffer's dialectic and similarly throws it out of balance. Bonhoeffer insists that personal longings must be relatively independent of Christ in some sense, and yet ultimately related to him as counterpoints to a pervasive theme. None of the authors cited above acknowledge the relative independence of personal longings from the person of Christ, nor its implications for the Christian way of life.

Bonhoeffer's call to a "life without God", therefore, is, in fact, less radical in meaning than his secular interpreters at first believed. But it is far more provocative than present scholars appreciate. For through the lens of his work on secular desires, we see Bonhoeffer encouraging a profound worldliness, a devotion to earthly life for its own sake, urged on the believer by God Himself. This call to full life without God, and yet before God, poses important questions for Bonhoeffer's anthropology and ethics as well. The issue which prompts this study, therefore, is one which the present author feels is new, unexplored, and significant to the broader endeavor of Bonhoeffer scholarship.

This inquiry will begin with an analysis of Bonhoeffer's treatment of secular desires in the Letters and Papers from Prison. We will note the originality of Bonhoeffer's position on human longings, and raise several questions which it generates. It will be argued that Bonhoeffer's account of purely human, earthly desires is in sharp contrast to any of his work before 1939. The contrast may appear to entail a contradiction, but I do not take it to be such, and will not argue the case. For our purposes it will be sufficient to claim that Bonhoeffer encourages and urges earthly desires straightforwardly in the Letters, and that before 1939 he wrote nothing comparable.

To account for this change of position, I will appeal first to the Bonhoeffer biography, noting the increasing sense of deprivation which Bonhoeffer experienced in pre-war Germany. Many of life's good things and pleasures, to which he had been accustomed, ebbed from his life and he found himself in the unfamiliar position of longing for loved ones and for the simple joys of life which he had taken for granted. At the same time, Bonhoeffer began to devote himself more passionately to the good things of the earth. His love for Maria, his recognition of the profound value of his friendship with Eberhard Bethge, and, politically, his decision to take part in the resistance movement, are examples of this personal development. In short, Bonhoeffer admittedly experienced, for the first time, the richness, value and importance of earthly desires, and began to offer a theological account of his experience in his later writings. Particular attention will be paid to the events surrounding his visit to, and swift return from, New York in 1939. It will be argued that his truncated visit produced a crisis and turning-point in Bonhoeffer's life and led him to an awareness of the profound longings which, in large part, prompted his return to Germany. From the time of that "crisis" until his death, Bonhoeffer exhibited a growing interest in the phenomenon of earthly desires which culminated in his explicit affirmation of their value for the Christian in the Letters.

The focus of the study will be upon the Ethics, Bonhoeffer's first drafts for his magnum opus, composed between the winter of 1939/1940 and his arrest in the spring of 1943. Selected portions of the Ethics will be examined in chronological sequence in order to see what value, if any, he assigns to earthly reality, and how he depicts fallen life "without God". For if he ascribes value to fallen life in some form, this will clarify how he is later able to encourage secular desires for the "good" things of the earth for their own sake. Since there is no evidence to the contrary, it will be assumed as a working hypothesis that Bonhoeffer thinks consistently, if also progressively, over the five years during which he wrote the Ethics and the Letters. Therefore, whenever a correlation can be logically inferred between the two texts, I will take the parallel to be in Bonhoeffer's mind, whether or not he explicitly states the connection himself. In this manner, I hope to verify and confirm both the continuity of the Letters with the Ethics and also the original position on earthly life found in these later texts.

Since there is a lack of secondary materials speaking directly to the subject of our inquiry, we will refer to other sources only occasionally, for guidance in matters of biography, for arguments which run counter to our own, and for support at related points in our analysis. For the most part, however, the study will remain as close to Bonhoeffer's text as possible. In this way, we intend to allow Bonhoeffer to speak largely for himself on the subject of earthly desires.

Our concluding chapter will present a survey of our findings. Those assertions from the Letters that are unique to the Bonhoeffer of 1939-1945 will be stated along with claims from the Ethics which clarify and expand their meaning. Taken together, these propositions will establish, as nearly as possible, what Bonhoeffer intended when he encouraged a life "without God before God". In particular, we will focus upon one form of Christian devotion to, and desiring of, fallen earthly life, namely, personal longings for absent loved ones.

It is hoped that this study will, in some measure, illuminate the thought of Dietrich Bonhoeffer and advance the course of research into his work. If it succeeds in some clarifying of his subtlety, suggesting to others the direction of his fertile mind, or raising questions which others will pursue, then the purpose of this effort will have been fulfilled to my satisfaction.

Notes to Introduction

[1] Dietrich Bonhoeffer, Letters and Papers from Prison (enlarged edition, New York: Macmillan Paperback, 1972), p. 303.

[2] Dietrich Bonhoeffer, Life Together, translated with an Introduction by John W. Doberstein from the German Gemeinsames Leben (Munich: Christian Kaiser Verlag, 1939), New York: Harper and Row, 1954, p. 31.

[3] Dietrich Bonhoeffer, "Thy Kingdom Come!" translated in John D. Godsey, ed., Preface to Bonhoeffer (Philadephia: Fortress Press, 1965), p. 32.

[4] Thomas Day, in his book Dietrich Bonhoeffer on Christian Community and Common Sense (Lewiston, New York: Edwin Mellen Press, 1982), p. 193, refers to this theme in passing. However, since his own work examines other dimensions of Bonhoeffer's thought, he does not pursue the issue in any detail.

[5] W. W. Bartley III, "The Bonhoeffer Revival", The New York Review of Books, II (August 26, 1965).

[6] The principal works of the authors cited are as follows: Thomas Altizer, The Gospel of Christian Atheism (Philadelphia: Westminster Press, 1966); William Hamilton, Radical Theology and the Death of God (Indianapolis: Bobbs-Merrill, 1966); Paul Van Buren, The Secular Meaning of the Gospel (New York: Macmillan, 1963); John A.T. Robinson, Honest to God (Philadelphia: Westminster Press, 1963). For a more complete bibliography see Toward a New Christianity: Readings in the Death of God Theology, ed. Thomas Altizer (New York: Harcourt, Brace & World, Inc., 1967), pp. 365-374.

[7] E. L. Mascall, The Secularization of Christianity (London: Darton, Longmans, and Todd, 1965). p. 120.

[8] Letters, pp. 327, 328.

[9] John A.T. Robinson, Honest to God (Philadelphia: The Westminster Press, 1963), pp. 38, 39.

[10] See Paul Van Buren's "Bonhoeffer's Paradox" in Bonhoeffer in a World Come of Age, ed. Peter Vorkink (Philadelphia: Fortress Press, 1968), pp. 23, 24.

[11]Each of these works is cited at the close of this study.

[12]David Hopper, in his <u>Dissent on Bonhoeffer</u> (Philadelphia: West- minster Press, 1975), argues that the inability of these authors to achieve consensus on the pervasive themes in Bonhoeffer's work indicates that no systematic coherence is there to be found. James Patrick Kelley takes up this charge in his <u>Revelation and the Secular in the Theology of Dietrich Bonhoeffer</u> (Ann Arbor, Michigan: University Microfilms International, 1980), and it is to his debate with Hopper that we direct the reader (see especially Kelley's pages 10-13 and 74-85). While we side with Kelley, the issue is not central to the course of our inquiry.

[13]<u>Kelley</u>, p. 5.

[14]In January of 1929, Bonhoeffer gave an address to his congregation entitled "What is a Christian Ethic?" Here he speaks of the believer's commitment to the earth: "But through this freedom from the law, from principle, the Christian must enter into the complexity of the world...He remains earthbound, even when his desire is towards God; he must go through all the anxiety before the laws of the world; he must learn the paradox that the world offers us a choice, not between good and evil, but between one evil and another, and that nevertheless God leads him to himself even through evil. He must feel the gross contradiction between what he would like to do and what he must do; he must grow mature through this distress, grow mature through not leaving hold of God's hand in the words 'Thy will be done'. A glimpse of eternity is revealed only through the depths of our earth, only through the storms of a human conscience. The profound old saga tells of the giant Antaeus, who was stronger than any man on earth; no one could overcome him until once in a fight someone lifted him from the ground; then the giant lost all the strength which had flowed into him through his contact with the earth. The man who would leave the earth, who would depart from the present distress, loses the power which still holds him by eternal, mysterious forces. The earth remains our mother, just as God remains our Father, and our mother will only lay in the Father's arms him who remains true to her. That is the Christian's song of earth and her distress". See <u>No Rusty Swords</u> (New York: Harper and Row, 1965), pp. 39-48. It is important to note here that Bonhoeffer does not affirm the fallen, earthly pole of life here <u>in itself</u>. He lives the earthly paradox for the sake of God, not for the sake of the life itself. It is not until after 1939 that Bonhoeffer explicitly affirms the relative goodness of natural life and encourages the believer to desire

those earthly goods for their own sakes, in relative independence from Christ. These affirmations are absent from the Barcelona address.

[15]Bonhoeffer claims that he is doing something new in Christian theology at several important junctures in the development of his argument. In Chapter IV of the Ethics, for example, he describes the situation in Western Christendom with respect to the understanding of the ultimate and penultimate, and concludes that many "do not clearly perceive, or at any rate, do not resolutely accept, the connection of the penultimate with the ultimate..." Therefore, he argues, a revised account of their relationship is required: "What must be done... is to fortify the penultimate with a more emphatic proclamation of the ultimate, and also to protect the ultimate by taking due care for the penultimate" (p. 142). Bonhoeffer's conclusion, that the penultimate is to be taken seriously in its own way, respected and validated in the light of the ultimate (pp. 140-142) leads him to his novel discussion of the natural. Here, Bonhoeffer explicitly states that the concept of the natural has "fallen into discredit in Protestant ethics" (p. 143), and that this "disastrous mistake" (p. 143) and "serious and substantial loss to Protestant thought" must be corrected. But the view of the natural he introduces is new to Catholic as well as Protestant thought. He specifically argues that the natural is not preliminary to life in Christ, nor is it in some sense continuous with the ultimate. As he states in a footnote, it differs from the Catholic perspective in that "1) we regard reason as having been entirely involved in the Fall, while according to Catholic dogmatics reason still retained a certain essential integrity, and 2) according to the Catholic doctrine, reason may also grasp the formal determination of the natural, the second of these principles being connected with the first" (p. 146). Bonhoeffer knows that his position is foreign to Protestant thought, and fundamentally divergent from the Catholic notion of the natural. He insists, therefore, that he is introducing a new perspective to Christian thought.

Later, in Chapter V, Bonhoeffer reviews the history of two-realm thinking in Christian thought, and argues for the abandonment of this conception: "Since the beginnings of Christian ethics after the times of the New Testament the main underlying conception in ethical thought, and the one which consciously or unconsciously has determined its whole course, has been the conception of a juxtaposition and conflict of two spheres, the one divine, holy, supernatural and Christian, and the other worldly, profane, natural and un-Christian... Reality as a whole now falls into two parts, and the concern of ethics is with the proper relation of these two parts to each other... It may be difficult to break the spell of this thinking in terms of two spheres, but it is nevertheless quite certain that it is in profound contradiction to the thought of the Bible and to the thought of the Reformation" (pp. 196, 197).

Bonhoeffer often makes appeal to the New Testament and to Luther, as well, arguing that the restoration of New Testament insights in Luther was often subverted in Lutheran orthodoxy, or "pseudo-Lutheranism" as he occasionally calls it. For a few such examples, see the Ethics, pages 142-144, 199, 231, 232, 253, 255, 256, and 263.

These examples are significant for our inquiry, because Bonhoeffer's praise and encouragement of personal longings is made possible by his insistence upon the relative independence and validity of the secular. Bonhoeffer's novel views of the penultimate, the natural, and earthly life as unified in the reconciliation of Jesus Christ establish the foundation for his later call in the Letters to living multi-dimensional, polyphonous life "as if there were no God".

CHAPTER I
DIETRICH BONHOEFFER'S
ENCOURAGEMENT OF HUMAN LOVE:
A RADICAL SHIFT IN HIS LATER THEOLOGY

The desire for the good things of the earth, particularly the longing to be with others, becomes a central motif in Bonhoeffer's writings after 1939. In the last years of his life, Bonhoeffer devoted careful attention to the demands, frustrations and rewards which accompany strong feelings, and frequently advanced a thesis which he never affirmed in his earlier work. He now repeatedly encourages and urges Christians to desire the good things of the earth for their own sake. As we shall see, Bonhoeffer is referring to such things as human play, bodily pleasures, friendship, family intimacy and, in particular, the bliss and solace which two people in love experience in being together. After 1939, Bonhoeffer claims that these earthly realities should be desired by the Christian in a certain abstraction from and relative independence of all other realities such as duties, responsibilities, and even such as God and Jesus Christ. This position is new to his own thought, provocative and untraditional.

The thesis receives extended treatment in Bonhoeffer's Letters and Papers from Prison. In this chapter, we will analyze how Bonhoeffer praises and encourages secular desires in the prison writings, and the grounds he gives for this positive assessment. Then we will pose several questions which this account raises, and turn to the pre-1939 corpus for clarification. Finding no encouragement and urging of secular longings in the writings prior to 1939, we will seek answers to our questions in our subsequent analysis of the Ethics.

Bonhoeffer did not consider the question of earthly desires in prison solely because he was deprived of life's good things and separated from his loved ones. It resulted also from the fact that during his last years, Bonhoeffer's life ceased to be purely matter-of-fact and task-oriented. He began to experience deep, personal longings, and to value their importance and richness in human life. In prison, Bonhoeffer admitted that his own life had lacked the desires for earthly joys he now appreciated. Thoughts of duty and of the purposefulness of his actions had deprived him of the yearning for life's pleasures which he now recognized as essential to the fullfillment of one's humanness, and even one's Christianity. His own emphasis upon the "ethical" and the corresponding loss of spontaneity and yearnings had exacted a toll upon him:

> At any rate, I must say that I myself have
> lived for many, many years quite absorbed in
> aims and tasks and hopes without any personal
> longing;  and perhaps that has made me old
> before my time.  It has made everything too

> "matter-of-fact." ...we can be very glad when
> something affects us deeply and regard the
> accompanying pain as enrichment.[1]

Again, Bonhoeffer did not brood over his desires solely because of the negative experience of prison life, but also because he
had come to know the richness and value of personal longings in his
own life. Yet the painful reality of his prison life was that he was
virtually alone, deprived of those whom he loved and needed. In the
midst of his isolation, he wrote that "the centre of our lives is outside
ourselves..." in others, and that people and relationships are more
important than anything else in life.[2] The persistent longings for the
life he had known before his imprisonment, and the life he hoped for
after his imprisonment, (e.g. his marriage with Maria) combined
with the ample time at his disposal, provided Bonhoeffer the occasion
and the opportunity to try to understand his earthly longings. His
yearnings for those he could not see or touch prompted him to ponder
the hopes, disappointments, despair, memories, and even fantasies
which he described in the poems "Who Am I?", "The Past", and
elsewhere in his letters.[3] These feelings threatened to draw him out
of the present into the past or into an imagined, unreal future. His
task, as he discovered it, was to keep alive the intensity of the feelings
he had come to value, and yet to do so in manner which freed him to
be fully human and loving in the present. But his sufferings and
longings for the good things of the earth were so intense, so painful,
that Bonhoeffer often asked if they were worth the agony they
produced.[4] In order to endure the anguish and to continue to feel the
full weight of his yearnings, Bonhoeffer found that he needed the
assurance that Christians, by their faith, were somehow encouraged
by God, indeed commanded, to want the good things of the earth for
their own sake. This led to his second, theological task which was to
justify such ardent desires as valuable in themselves, as Bonhoeffer
had experienced them, devoid though they often are of thoughts of
God.

In the analysis which follows, we will examine Bonhoeffer's
attempt to carry out this dual task. As we will see, his statements
are primarily experiential and practical in nature, but their
theological content is in striking contrast with the theological
statements on corresponding themes written before 1939. We will
examine this contrast and its significance and raise questions
requiring further clarification.

In the <u>Letters</u> <u>and</u> <u>Papers</u> <u>from</u> <u>Prison</u>, Bonhoeffer argues
that God wants the believer to love him in such a way that his

passionate, sensual love has its full independence, unrestrainedly developing into its own fullness.[5] At every wedding, he writes, one should rejoice at the sight of two persons boldly forging a future grounded in their desire for mutual joy. Their shared desire for earthly happiness is their own choice, their own accomplishment, and they are right to be proud of it: "We ought not to be in too much of a hurry here to speak piously of God's will and guidance".[6] The earthly bliss which they desire in mutually comforting one another in body and soul is the object of their own will and longing. God is not the source of their desire: it is their own. Their earthly, secular desire is justified in itself, though relatively independent of the purposes of God. But God does add his "Yes" to their love, a "Yes" to their desire for one another. Through marriage, God endorses and encourages their wish to be with one another into the future.

A Christian bride and groom, therefore, rightly desire their happiness for its own sake, in a certain abstraction and independence from God. The independence, however, is only relative. Although the wedding is the achievement and victory of the bride and groom, their will toward that achievement is only made possible by the will and guidance of God. Their love desires only the heaven of their own happiness, but their faith understands and accepts God's purposes for them in the estate of mat- rimony. Through marriage, God assigns them a post of responsibility, linking them into the chain of generations which serves to preserve and perpetuate the human race.[7]

We observe throughout the letters a striking affirmation of the value of human desires, and a stress upon the Christian's rightful desire for life itself and for the good things of the earth. Believers are urged to love the earth so deeply that they yearn for and seek out its good things.[8] Our love for the good things of the earth also compels us to seek their preservation.[9] It is not the Christian's calling to neglect or minimize these earthly longings by thinking instead of higher, spiritual matters or of their eternal home. To look beyond the good thing desired deprives one of the full happiness conveyed by the things in itself.

> I believe that we ought to love and trust God in our lives [emphasis is Bonhoeffer's], and in all the good things that he sends us, that when the time comes (but not before!) we may go to him with love, trust and joy. But, to put it plainly, for a man in his wife's arms to be hankering after the other world is, in mild terms, a piece

4

of bad taste, and not God's will. We ought to
find and love God in what he actually gives us;
if it pleases him to allow us to enjoy some
overwhelming earthly happiness, we musn't try
to be more pious than God himself and allow
our happiness to be corrupted by presumption
and arrogance, and by unbridled religious fan-
tasy which is never satisfied with what God
gives. God will see to it that the man who
finds him in his earthly happiness and thanks
him for it does not lack reminders that earthly
things are transient, that it is good for him to
attune his heart to what is eternal, and that
sooner or later there will be times when he
can say in all sincerity, "I wish I were home."
But everything has its time.[10]

This affirmation of the Christian's rightful desire for the good
things of the earth enables Bonhoeffer to urge believers to immerse
themselves in the pleasures of life for their own sake. While he
writes at some length on the desire of lovers for one another, the
shared life of lovers is only one example of the earthly happiness
which the Christian is encouraged to enjoy. Friendship, also, the
"finest and rarest blossom",[11] and "most precious good (kostbarste
Gut)"[12] develops from "the spirit's choice and free desire".[13] In a
freer, less earthly way than the sexual love of man and woman,
friendship draws two people together as one. It offers comfort,
strength, refuge and happiness, a haven of trust in the midst of life's
turbulence.[14] God establishes an area of freedom (Spielraum) for
Christians to devote themselves to friends, play, music, art,
education and enjoyment. This "broad area of freedom" sets us free
for pleasure, for joy. It is a freedom to enjoy life and others without
impeding life's flow. The person who remains ignorant of this realm
of freedom for the exercise of earthly desire is the poorer for it: "I
doubt whether he is a complete man and therefore a Christian in the
widest sense of the term".[15]

Bonhoeffer writes in a similar spirit to his mother. As she
celebrates her birthday "in a large circle of family and friends with
joy and thankfulness", he is reminded of the freedom enjoyed by the
Christian to seek out the pleasures of life:

The time between Easter and Ascension has
always been particularly important to me. Our
gaze is already directed to the last thing of

all, but we still have our tasks, our joys and
our sorrows on this earth and the power of
living is granted to us by Easter. I say nothing
but what I have experienced when I thank you
today for going before us on this way between
Easter and Ascension; it is the blessing that
father and Max have left behind for you and for
us. I too want to go this way with Maria, quite
prepared for the last thing, for eternity, and
yet wholly present for the tasks, the beauties
and troubles of this earth. Only in this way
can we be completely happy and completely at
peace together. We want to receive what God
bestows on us with open, outstretched hands
and delight in it with all our hearts and with a
quiet heart we will sacrifice what God does
not yet grant us or takes away from us...[16]

In these passages, Bonhoeffer clearly argues that realities of
earthly life are often truly "values", "good" and "beautiful", distinct
from any union with God, and that the Christian can experience
them as such. In short, Bonhoeffer affirms here the intrinsic value
of certain earthly realities in themselves. Bonhoeffer, therefore, calls
upon the Christian to seek human, earthly joys and urges the
Church likewise to encourage the believer's pursuit of these good
things of life:

I wonder whether it is possible (it almost
seems so today) to regain the idea of the
church as providing an understanding of the
area of freedom (art, education, friendship,
play), so that Kierkegaard's "aesthetic existence" would not be banished from the church's
sphere, but would be re-established within
it?... Who is there, for instance, in our times,
who can devote himself with an easy mind to
music, friendship, games or happiness? Surely
not the "ethical man", but only the Christian.[17]

Bonhoeffer discovered, however, that when one feels strongly,
a painful, existential tension is generated which is not easily borne.
Nowhere does Bonhoeffer express this tension as poignantly as he
does in the poems "Who Am I?" and "The Past". In "Who Am I?" he
expresses the wretchedness of his isolation from the good things of
life:

6

Am I then really all that which other men tell of?
Or am I only what I know of myself,
restless and longing and sick, like a bird in a cage,
struggling for breath, as though hands were compressing my throat,
yearning for colours, for flowers, for the voices of birds,
thirsting for words of kindness, for neighborliness,
trembling with anger at despotisms and petty humiliation,
tossing in expectation of great events,
powerlessly trembling for friends at an infinite distance,
weary and empty at praying, at thinking, at making,
faint, and ready to say farewell to it all?[18]

In "The Past" he focuses upon the suffering which attends the longing for loved ones.

O happiness beloved, and pain beloved in heaviness,
   you went from me.
What shall I call you?  Anguish, life, blessedness,
part of myself, my heart -- the past?
The door was slammed;
I hear your steps depart and slowly die away.
What now remains for me -- torment, delight, desire?
This only do I know:  that with you, all has gone.
But do you feel how I now grasp at you
and so clutch hold of you
that it must hurt you?
How I so rend you
that your blood gushes out,
simply to be sure that you are near me,
a life in earthly form, complete?
Do you divine my terrible desire
for my own suffering,
my eager wish to see my own blood flow,
only that all may not go under,
lost in the past?
Life, what have you done to me?
Why did you come?  Why did you go?[19]

In "Who Am I?" Bonhoeffer speaks of the despair which haunts him, a persistent desire to "say farewell to it all". The pain of his yearning often seems unbearable. Yet, in "The Past", he writes of his refusal to give up, preferring the agony of his longings to the loss of his past. Somehow, Bonhoeffer's desires are worth the pain, for they help preserve the riches of life he has known. Thus, while forced to live without his loved ones and without access to the full range of life's gifts, Bonhoeffer found that desiring the good things of the earth for their own sake was not a simple matter. While many think it easy to desire earthly realities, Bonhoeffer experienced it differently. He found desiring to be agony. As his words suggest, a cruel tension accompanies genuine yearning, along with the prospect of further pain and frustration.

The unwillingness of many Christians to face such unpleasant prospects, to bear the attendant anxiety and misery, keeps them from "real desires". Bonhoeffer urges believers to feel their longings fully and thereby experience the richness of abundant life. The idea that Christians should avoid desires and their accompanying pleasures and pains, however lofty the motivation, is rejected on both theological and humanistic grounds.

> To renounce a full life and its real joys in order to avoid pain is neither Christian nor human...[20]

> Lack of desire is poverty...[21]

> When you've deliberately suppressed every desire for so long, it may have one of two bad results: either it burns you up inside, or it gets so bottled up that one day there is a terrific explosion...[22]

Others become too involved in life's duties to desire life's good things. They refuse to exert the effort demanded to feel their longing fully:

> Almost everyone has aims and tasks, and everything is objectified, reified to such a tremendous extent -- how many people today allow themselves any strong personal feeling and real yearning, or take the trouble to spend their strength freely in working out and carrying out that yearning, and letting it bear fruit?[23]

The English translator has Bonhoeffer speak of people "not allowing" themselves strong desires, but the German is more accurately rendered as "not achieving" (leisten) strong desires. Powerful desires are not achieved by the giving-up of oneself to yearnings, but are an accomplishment, requiring great personal strength. Most people never achieve strong desires; Bonhoeffer dryly notes that most are at best capable of identifying with "sentimental radio hits" whose "artificial naivete and empty crudities" are but a "ghastly desolation and impoverishment".[24] Sentiment such as this is not indicative of strong feelings.

Bonhoeffer compared his experience of longing with the desires of those around him in prison. They, too, were separated from those they loved, and they also yearned to be with them. But there was a striking difference in the nature of their desires. Unlike Bonhoeffer, when they desired, they were "all desire".[25] They were overcome by the flood of their own feelings and rendered unable to act responsibly or to care for others. They became so engrossed in their feelings that they were no longer present for the demands and needs of the moment. It is noteworthy that Bonhoeffer does not criticize these feelings because they have been allowed to grow too strong, but rather because they are too weak. People thus dominated and virtually incapacitated by their yearnings are said to lack strong feelings. Their passion is weak, limited, and ultimately unfulfilling.

This presents us with a paradox. In what sense can a desire be said to be weak which fills our consciousness and sweeps us along with it? Such a desire would appear, at least, to be extraordinarily potent. Bonhoeffer clarifies this for us in his discussion on the "mastering" of desires. Those who cling to their desires obsessively and are dominated by them have failed to master them. The result is that the desires hinder the expression on one's full humanity and negatively affect one's capacity to function as a mature individual. As a corollary, Bonhoeffer explains that the mastering of desires makes people more whole, stronger, more compassionate, and prepared for the exigencies of the present.

> There is a wholeness about the fully grown
> man which enables him to face an existing
> situation squarely. He may have his longings,
> but he keeps them out of sight and somehow
> masters them... desires repeatedly mastered
> for the sake of present duty make us richer...
> It's remarkable then how others come to rely
> on us, confide in us, and let us talk to them.[26]

When one masters his desires, desires are said to be "strong", "full" and "unrestrained". But the question may still be posed: If a desire is mastered, how can it be said to grow stronger? The person may grow stronger and act with greater strength by mastering his desires, but would not the mastering of a desire serve to weaken the desire itself?

Bonhoeffer's own practice in the mastering of his desires is illuminating. One familiar with the Christian tradition would expect him to master his desires by turning his thoughts away from his longings to "higher", spiritual concerns. Or he might tame the desire by feeding it dreams of its eventual satisfaction, and rest content with that. But Bonhoeffer rejects both of these alternatives. Both are illusory. The only way to master desires, he insists, is to face them head-on and feel them fully. One must not settle for otherworldly hopes or this-worldly replacements and distractions. One must not seek substitutes of any kind:

> ...there is nothing worse in such times than to
> try to find a substitute for the irreplaceable.
> It just does not work, and it leads to still
> greater indiscipline, for the strength to over-
> come tension (such strength can only come
> from looking the longing straight in the face)
> is impaired, and endurance becomes even more
> unbearable...[27]

> First, nothing can make up for the absence of
> someone whom we love, and it would be wrong
> to try to find a substitute; we must simply
> hold out and see it through. That sounds very
> hard at first, but at the same time it is a great
> consolation, for the gap, as long as it remains
> unfilled, preserves the bounds between us...[28]

When one concentrates fully upon the one desired, a number of positive things result. The bond of fellowship between the lover and the loved one is preserved and strengthened, one finds a certain strength to master the desire, and one also enjoys the rich experience of remembering the good things of the past and looking ahead to the promise of joys to come. The wealth of one's experience unfolds in the concentrated effort to feel personal longings deeply and fully.

Bonhoeffer often insists that when his or her desire is fulfilled the Christian is to enjoy it to the fullest.[29] But he does not speak of mastering desires in this context. He speaks of it instead when he is concerned with unsatisfied yearnings, frustrated hopes. One masters such desires, he says, by concentrating fully on the object of desire. One squarely confronts the good thing or person that is missed, and refuses the consolation of substitutes: "We simply have to wait and wait; we have to suffer unspeakably from the separation and feel the longing till it makes us ill".[30]

For Bonhoeffer there is no choice whether or not he will desire fully. He "has to".[31] First of all, yearning preserves a kind of union (Gemeinschaft) with the absent ones we love. The fellowship once known is brought vividly to mind in desire, and strengthened, so that the bonds between people are maintained. The "gap", as he describes the absence of a loved one, "so long as it stays really unfilled, keeps us bound together".[32] We have to hold out (aushalten und durchhalten) in feeling fully the absence of our loved one.

But why do we need this union with those we love? Why do we desire it so violently and persistently? It is not because of our Christian faith, Bonhoeffer argues, although God assists in keeping the hole empty and the bond intact. Nor does the necessity come from morality. It comes instead from our "nature". This is why substitutes just "disgust us" (widert uns an).[33] We simply cannot turn away from our desires for our loved ones.

To pursue the question further, what is it in our nature which drives us incessantly towards those we love, and into the strenuous task of having to master our desires? For Bonhoeffer, the answer lies in the notion of life itself. He links no other theme so consistently with earthly desire as that of "life". As he explains it, it is basic to human nature that people want to live, and to be happy,[34] so we naturally experience intense feelings for loved ones and for the good things of the earth. We naturally desire things which bring us joy. These desires, whether fulfilled or unfulfilled, enrich us,[35] enhance our humanness, and enable us to enjoy a whole and abundant life.[36] They are desires to which we have a right, for they improve the quality of our lives and assist us in "being what we ought to be and can be..."[37]

When these desires are mastered, an order or discipline is established in human life,[38] for individual desires which are fully felt help to establish a natural harmony within the larger movement of our lives. The fullness and multi-dimensionality of our lives are intimately related to the fullness of our desires. It is somehow natural that desires assume a particular form, and the extent to which this takes place determines the character of life. The "strength" to be found in desires appears related to a power of life itself straining to convey to us the appropriate, life-fulfilling form to give to our desires. Again, Bonhoeffer does not state this explicitly.

Instead, he argues consistently from experience that mastered desires improve and enrich one's life, and that unmastered desires erode life's fullness. It is natural and beneficial to feel desires fully, and unnatural and harmful not to.

Only mastered desires, then, those that have developed completely and appropriately, enrich Christian faith and life. This requires expending effort and strength "to bring a desire to term (ausautragen), to work it out, and to let it bear its fruits".[39] A desire must bear its fruits, no more. The "hot, sensual, burning love" of the Song of Songs, for example, though deeply passionate and unbridled, is a part of life's flow when it is permitted to develop "as powerfully as possible" and remains a distinct whole, wholly for itself (ein eigenes, ganzes, ganz fur sich).[40] It would appear that the thrust of desires is to be fully themselves, to mature as life's forms. Apparently, no single desire is to become our sole desire, nor subsume all of life under its rule. A desire strives only to be one of many, but it strives to be full.

Bonhoeffer concluded from his own experiences that fallen life was not strong enough in itself to achieve the full development of its many forms. Without the assistance of faith, fallen human beings cannot exert the effort and discipline necessary to gain command over their passions. They succumb to either an unnatural repression or avoidance of desire, or weakly permit desires to overrun their lives. Some have undergone much suffering in the experience of yearning, and retreat as a result from the effort required to master their desires.

> In my experience nothing tortures us more than
> longing. Some people have been so violently
> shaken in their lives from their earliest days
> that they cannot, so to speak, allow them-
> selves any great longing or put up with a long
> period of tension, and they find compensation
> in shortlived pleasures that offer readier sat-
> isfaction... It's not true to say that it is good
> for a man to have suffered heavy blows early
> and often in life; in most cases it breaks him.
> True, it hardens people for times like ours, but
> it also greatly helps to deaden them.[41]

Others simply lack the power to master their desires, although they try. Their desires overcome them. Their failure, too, deprives them of a measure of their full humanness:

Almost all the people that I find in my present
surroundings cling to their own desires, and so
have no interest in others; they no longer
listen and they're incapable of loving their
neighbour.[42]

Since fallen human beings are unable to face their desires
and feel them fully without repressing them or clinging to them
obsessively, it follows that they are particularly unsuited to the task of
mastering the onslaught of multiple longings. When one is beseiged
by several yearnings at once, one can only resort to the unsuccessful
methods he or she has adopted in the attempt to master individual
desires. The result is a predictable and resounding failure:

I notice repeatedly here how few people there
are who can harbour conflicting emotions at
the same time. When bombers come, they are
all fear; when there is something nice to eat,
they are all greed; when they are disap-
pointed, they are all despair; when they are
successful, they can think of nothing else.
They miss the fullness of life and the wholeness of independent existence; everything objective and subjective is dissolved for them
into fragments.[43]

Bonhoeffer argues that in order for us to experience the multi-
dimensionality of life we must learn to master our desires. As a first
step in getting people out of their one-track minds, he states that they
must be taught to think.

What a deliverance it is to be able to think,
and thereby remain multi-dimensionality. I've
almost made it a rule here, simply to tell
people who are trembling under an air raid that
it would be much worse for a small town. We
have to get people out of their one-track
minds; that is a kind of 'preparation' for faith,
or something that makes faith possible,
although really it's only faith itself that can
make possible a multi-dimensional life...[44]

Bonhoeffer implies that reason reveals life's variety and complexity;
thus, he reminds those in the midst of an air raid of the multi-di-

13

mensionality of life, of other people, other needs, other possible circumstances. This perspective on their fears can help people place their desires into the larger context of human experience and perhaps enable them to face them more fully, neither refusing to feel them nor overemphasizing their significance. Such a perspective on life can help them master their fear. Still, escaping from the prison of "one-track minds" is not sufficient to equip one for full, multi-dimensional living. It may "prepare" one for faith in providing a foretaste of such living, but reason by itself is incapable of establishing a full, polyphonous life.

For this, one needs the cantus firmus, or the love of God, to bring the tones of one's life together into polyphonous harmony. A cantus firmus, as the term is used in music, is the principal voice or melodic theme subject to contrapuntal treatment. It is in relation to the cantus firmus that the counterpoints can be developed to their limits, in one sense independently of the theme, yet in another sense ultimately reliant upon it.[45] For the Christian, the cantus firmus, the paramount love, is love for God:

> What I mean is that God wants us to love him
> eternally with our whole hearts -- not in such
> a way as to injure or weaken our earthly love,
> but to provide a kind of cantus firmus to which
> the other melodies of life provide the counter-
> point. One of these contrapuntal themes
> (which have their own complete independence
> but are yet related to the cantus firmus) is
> earthly affection.[46]

The Christian's love for God brings joy to the daily life of faith, and fosters a longing to be with the object of devotion and love into eternity. It also generates a fundamental trust in the loving presence of God in the midst of life, a basic assurance that "nothing calamitous can happen as long as the cantus firmus is kept going".[47] It is a consuming love, a desire which persists throughout and undergirds the life of the believer. Thus, the Christian's love for God serves as the cantus firmus for all the contrapuntal desires of human life. One needs the love of God to promote the full expression of all the dimensions of one's life.

> ...Christianity puts us into many different di-
> mensions of life at the same time; we make
> room for ourselves, to some extent, for God
> and the whole world. We rejoice with those

14

who rejoice, and weep with those who weep;
we are anxious... about our life, but at the
same time we must think about things much
more important to us than life itself.... Life
isn't pushed back into a single dimension, but
is kept multi-dimensional and polyphonous.[48]

The cantus firmus sets earthly desires free to become full and
relatively independent, and yet ultimately reliant upon it. Through
their relationship with the cantus firmus, desires can develop fully
and perfectly, and yet in harmony with one another. Without the
cantus firmus, one cannot escape one-dimensionality and a fragmented life.

Bonhoeffer introduces this musical metaphor of the cantus
firmus in response to a letter from Bethge in which he described his
longing for Renate. Moved by Bethge's yearnings, Bonhoeffer
affirms his desiring and advises him on the attendant suffering:

...I can't completely escape the feeling that
there is a tension in you which you can't get
rid of completely, and so I would like to help
you as a brother. If a man loves, he wants to
live, to live above all, and hates everything
that represents a threat to his life. You hate
the recollection of the last weeks, you hate
the blue sky, because it reminds you of them,
you hate the planes, etc. You want to live with
Renate and be happy, and you have a good right
to that... There's always a danger in all strong,
erotic love that one may lose what I might call
the polyphony of life. I wanted to tell you to
have a good, clear "cantus firmus"; that is the
only way to a full and perfect sound, when the
counterpoint has a firm support and can't come
adrift or get out of tune, while remaining a
distinct whole in its own right.[49]

Bonhoeffer wished to remind Bethge that a firm grasp of the cantus
firmus would assist him in developing his affection for Renate to its
full integrity as a contrapuntal theme. Bonhoeffer is writing to
Bethge to assure him that his desire for Renate is valuable and good,
and that it is supported by God. Bethge is not to hate his separation
from Renate and despair of life, but must realize that his desires,
though unfulfilled and painful, help make his life rich and full. If

15

Bethge permits his unsatisfied desires to make him bitter toward life, he will threaten his own humanness and the character of his faith.[50]

But Bonhoeffer's explanation of how and why the cantus firmus offers such assistance is sketchy. Clearly the desires are felt without the benefit of the cantus firmus. Faith is not needed, for desires are felt by all persons. But Bonhoeffer seems to say that the cantus firmus provides a peculiar impetus and sustenance to earthly desires in allowing them to be mastered, to develop their own contrapuntal themes to the fullest. All desires are related in some manner to most fundamental of desires, the love of God. The cantus firmus represents the theme in connection with which other passions of life can be sounded in their full contrapuntal integrity.

Through the ever-present theme of the love of God, the other sounds of life can join together in polyphonous harmony. The single themes become a polyphony, the counterpoints each developed to their limits. When the sounds of life retain their contact with the cantus firmus each theme remains a "distinct whole in its own right",[51] but stays in tune. For Bethge, the challenge is to sound the theme of his earthly affection to its full resonance, careful to respect its integrity as a form of life with its own developmental dynamic, and careful also to harmonize with the cantus firmus. In this way, he will preserve life's polyphony. Should he fail to do so, as those lacking the cantus firmus, he will simply blare the single theme of his desire, destroying the polyphony of his own life and perhaps disrupting the harmony of others. A single theme can find its true value only in relation to the cantus firmus, and in the midst of other themes, in a polyphony. So it is with desires. Each possesses its own form and provides something unique to the rich tapestry of one's life. God, above all, wants us to live, so God assists us in the development of life's infinite forms.

God's wish that human life be full and rich helps to explain why God promotes desires through the cantus firmus, but Bonhoeffer in the Letters does not describe the precise manner in which this assistance is given. One suggestion he offers is in his comparison of the cantus firmus and its counterpoints to the "undivided and yet distinct" relationship of the two natures of Christ. He asks:

> May not the attraction and importance of poly-
> phony in music consist in its being a musical
> reflection of this Christological fact and
> therefore of our vita christiana?... Do you see

what I'm driving at?[52]

Bonhoeffer's concluding question suggests that this thoughts on the cantus firmus had not yet crystallized into systematic form; they remained in an early stage of development. He appears to be drawing an analogy between the person of Jesus, both divine and human, and the believer. As the son of God, Christ was unable to lapse into sinfulness or break from the higher purpose for which He became Incarnate. Yet, at the same time, this divine nature enabled him to be fully human and desire the persons and things of the earth. Through his divinity, Christ is able to show persons the meaning of true humanity. As Christ's divinity supported the full expression of His humanity, so the believer's love for God analogously sets him free for the pursuit of earth's good things. But Bonhoeffer does not pursue this analogy; he simply asserts that the love of God will somehow be the source of Bethge's strength as he struggles with the anguish of his unsatisfied yearnings. It must be so if he is to succeed in mastering them.[53]

A further difficulty surrounds the thoroughly secular nature of Bethge's passions and Bonhoeffer's specific support of their secularity. Bethge's longing for Renate was not, first of all, related in any conscious way to thoughts of God. He did not yearn for Renate's voice and touch in order to fulfill any higher calling. Bethge longed to be with Renate; he wanted the solace, the comfort and the pleasure that they would enjoy together. According to the definition of "secular" with which we began,[54] Bethge's desire is clearly secular in character, and yet it is precisely this desiring of Renate, for her own sake, which Bonhoeffer applauds in his wedding sermon to them of May, 1943:

> It is obvious, and should not be ignored, that it
> is your own very human wills that are at work
> here, celebrating their triumph; the course
> that you are taking at the outset is one that
> you have chosen for yourselves; what you have
> done and are doing is not, in the first place,
> something religious, but something quite secu-
> lar. So you yourselves, and you alone, bear the
> responsibility for what no one can take from
> you. Unless you can boldly say today: 'That is
> our resolve, our way,' you are taking refuge in
> a false piety. 'Iron and steel may pass away,
> but our love shall abide for ever.' That desire
> for earthly bliss, which you want to find in one

another, and in which, to quote the medieval
song, one is the comfort of the other body in
body and soul -- that desire is justified before
God and man.[55]

In the sermon, Bonhoeffer praises the single-mindedness of
their desire for one another. Absent from the desire are competing
thoughts of God. Bethge's desire for Renate was for her alone.
Thoughts of God would have constituted a false piety, a substitute.
Like the yearnings for the other good things of the earth which
Bonhoeffer had earlier endorsed, the desires to which he here
ascribes value are also secular in nature.

In summary, we see Bonhoeffer in the Letters and Papers
from Prison unambiguously urging and encouraging the believer to
desire the good things of the earth for their own sake, in relative
independence from God. The Christian's love of God (cantus firmus)
helps believers "master" their desires, or develop them to their full
independence and wholeness as secular, contrapuntal themes. But
this account of the life "without God", as manifested in personal
longings, raises a number of questions. Why is it good or valuable to
feel secular longings for loved ones? What does Bonhoeffer mean by
the notion of "good" in "good" things of the earth, when understood
in relative independence from God? Why does God want our erotic,
earthly yearnings to develop as powerfully as possible, to their full
independence and wholeness? Why is it important for Christians to
feel a full, complete passion for their loved ones? How does the
cantus firmus assist in the achieving of mastered desires? In what
sense is the desire of the Christian for a loved one a distinct entity
wholly for itself? In what sense is it independent of Christ and yet
related to Him? Finally, how does the mastering of purely secular
yearnings make us more fully human? In what follows, we will
examine Bonhoeffer's writing before 1939, seeking clarification of his
provocative claims regarding earthly longings.

As noted above, Bonhoeffer's praise and encouragement of
secular, personal longings is problematic because it is a major shift
in his thought. Prior to 1939, Bonhoeffer did not encourage purely
human, secular desires of loved ones for one another; instead, he
wrote only of their fallenness. He acknowledged such desires, and
recognized their role in the preservation of human community, but
he never encouraged this fellowship for its own sake or urged the
desires which generate it. Personal longings were permitted and
tolerated, but never encouraged for their own sake. In contrast to
their role in Bonhoeffer's prison writings, earthly desires are
referred to only sparingly before 1939 and, as this brief survey of his

18

earlier statements which follows will indicate, the positive tone of the Letters sharply contrasts with the thoughts expressed prior to 1939.

In his first work, Communion of Saints (1927), Bonhoeffer describes Christian love as the surrender of one's will to the other, as exemplified in the person of Christ. When "we are far from him", Bonhoeffer argues, "all our love is self-love".[56] Genuine love "demands that we should sacrifice our own interest",[57] and forfeit our self-will. It is selfless, where all the "love" of the world is self-love.[58] Neither Bethge's love for Renate nor Bonhoeffer's love for Maria is a selfless yearning, and neither is renunciatory in nature. Each wants more from his moments with his loved one than to give selflessly: in his later writings, Bonhoeffer explicitly urges such longings, and encourages the Christian to desire the pleasure he or she will experience in the presence of the loved one. In the Communion of Saints, Bonhoeffer offers no such encouragement.

Later, in Creation and Fall (1933), Bonhoeffer traces the desire of lovers for one another to its source, and concludes that yearnings of the sort experienced by Bethge are directly related to sin and would not be a part of life had humanity not fallen into disunion. Bonhoeffer does not deny this in the Letters, but nonetheless claims a relative value for personal longings. In Creation and Fall he discusses the advent of sexuality and presents only a negative account of the desires it spawns.

According to this earlier Bonhoeffer, the creation of Eve confronts Adam with a bodily reminder of his own limitedness which he initially accepts, with gladness, as the gracious gift of his creator. Adam's joy in his helpmeet and in his God is reflected in the nature of his sexuality. Sexuality prior to the fall is described as "the expression of the two-sidedness of being both an individual and being one with the other person ... it is nothing but the ultimate realization of our belonging to one another".[59] This "community of love" owes its existence to God, and devotes itself to God's worship; in this respect, the first man and woman constitute the original Church.

But this is not how sexuality is expressed in the fallen world. With the Fall, all is changed: "The community of love... has been torn to pieces by sexuality and become passion".[60] As Adam becomes like God, his relationship with Eve immediately erodes; their unity dissolves. Their authentic relation, established in the creation of Eve, crumbles into inauthenticity.[61] Because Adam no longer accepts his limitedness, the presence of Eve as his limit cannot be tolerated. She affronts his newly-grasped sense of equality with God, and represents a limitation imposed upon him by what he sees as a wrathful, envious God; thus, his love for her is transformed into resentment. From his new perspective, it is impossible for Adam to look upon Eve with his former love:

> Now the limit is no more grace, holding man
> in the unity of his creaturely and free love; it
> is discord. Man and woman are divided. This
> means two things. First of all, man makes
> sure of his share in the woman's body; more
> generally, one man makes use of his right to
> the other and puts forward his claim to the
> possession of the other, thereby denying and
> destroying the other person's creatureli-
> ness.[62]

Sexuality, as we experience it subsequent to the Fall, is self-will and hatred and every limit.[63]

> This avid passion of man for the other person
> first comes to expression in sexuality. This
> sexuality of the man who has transgressed his
> limit is the refusal to recognize any limit
> whatever; it is the boundless passion to be
> without a limit. Sexuality is the passionate
> hatred of every limit; it is arbitrariness to
> the highest degree, it is self-will, it is avid,
> impotent will for unity in the divided world....
> Sexuality desires the destruction of the other
> person as creature; it robs him of his crea-
> tureliness, violates him as well as his limit,
> hates grace.[64]

Characterizing sexuality as he does here, it is no surprise, then, that Bonhoeffer does not praise or encourage it, although he admits its necessity in marriage.[65]

The result, as Bonhoeffer expressed it in Life Together (1939), is that human love, or the desire of two persons for one another, bears no resemblance to the communal harmony which was man's before the Fall. A basic point of the work is the absolute unlikeness of spiritual and human love, spiritual and human reality, and spiritual and human community:

> The basis of all spiritual reality is the clear,
> manifest Word of God in Jesus Christ. The
> basis of all human reality is the dark, turbid
> urges and desires of the human mind. The
> basis of the community of the Spirit is truth;
> the basis of human community of spirit is desire.[66]

Human love, Bonhoeffer explains, seeks immediate intimacy with the one loved. It is unwilling to mediate the relationship through Christ, to love _for_ His sake, to seek out His purposes in and for the other. Instead, it longs for direct contact, seeking a fusion of the "I" and the "Thou" through which the other can be subjected to one's sphere of power and influence. In effect, the I-Thou relation is replaced by an I-It relation in which each wants the other for selfish ends. Human love wants to bind the other to itself, to control, to dominate and to rule.[67] Bonhoeffer describes the egocentricity which nourishes human desires as follows:

> Perhaps the contrast between spiritual and hu-
> man reality can be made most clear in the fol-
> lowing observation: Within the spiritual com-
> munity there is never, nor in any way, any
> 'immediate' relationship of one to another,
> whereas human community expresses a pro-
> found, elemental, human desire for community,
> for immediate contact with other human souls,
> just as in the flesh there is the urge for phys-
> ical merger with other flesh. Such desire of
> the human soul seeks complete fusion of I and
> Thou, whether this occurs in the union of love
> or, what is after all the same thing, in the
> forcing of another person into one's sphere of
> power and influence.[68]

By its very nature, human love is the desire for community it lacks in sin. As we will see in Chapter I of the Ethics, this theme is repeated in Bonhoeffer's discussion of shame.

Neither in Life Together nor in the earlier portions of the Ethics does Bonhoeffer suggest that purely human desires strength-en fellowship (Gemeinschaft) and bind persons together in a good way, a theme which he explicitly, and repeatedly, affirms in the Letters and Papers from Prison. In Life Together, Bonhoeffer ac-knowledges that, while human love builds Gemeinschaft in the relationships of marriage, family and friendship, this Gemeinschaft is limited by its fallenness and humanness. The community founded upon human love generates a disfigured caricature of distinctive Christian love.

> Here [in the midst of human community] is
> where the humanly strong person is in his
> element, securing for himself the admiration,
> the love, or the fear of the weak. Here human
> ties, suggestions, and bonds are everything,
> and in the immediate community of souls we
> have reflected the distorted image of every-
> thing that is originally and solely peculiar to
> community mediated through Christ.... Human
> love is directed to the other person for his
> own sake, spiritual love loves him for Christ's
> sake. Therefore, human love seeks direct
> contact with the other person; it loves him
> not as a free person but as one whom it binds
> to itself. It wants to gain, to capture by any
> means; it uses force. It desires to be
> irresistible, to rule.[69]

In the human community we seek immediacy with other people, and desire them for their own sake. Thus, human love lacks the selfless-ness characteristic of distinctive Christian love. Bonhoeffer tolerates human love and recognizes its preservative role in the formation of the human community, but he does not encourage the believer to desire other persons for their own sake.[70] The statements in Life Together are milder in tone than those in Creation and Fall, but Bonhoeffer does not yet explicitly praise and encourage secular, personal longings.

In The Cost of Discipleship (1937), desires for the things of the earth are described as "incompatible with allegiance to God".[71] Any longing to enjoy the things of the earth for their own sake represents a break with Christ, a disavowal of His reconciliatory work, and a refusal to acknowledge Him as the one who stands between the believer and all reality.

> We must face up to the truth that the call of
> Christ does set up a barrier between man and
> his natural life.... By virtue of his incarnation
> he has come between man and his natural life.
> There can be no turning back, for Christ bars

the way. By calling us he has cut us off from
all immediacy with the things of this world....
It is the call of Jesus... which effects in us
this complete breach from the world.[72]

Christian sanctification is advanced, not by the believer's
polyphonous mastery of earthly desires, but by his clean separation
from the world wherein Satan "rules and deals death".[73] The call to
the Christian's enjoyment of earthly goods for its own sake is said to
rest upon a major theological misunderstanding:

It is a theological error of the first magnitude
to exploit the doctrine of Christ the Mediator
so as to justify direct relationships with the
things of this world. It is sometimes argued
that if Christ is the Mediator he has borne all
the sin which underlies our direct relationships with the world and that he has justified
us in them.... The breach with the things of the
world is now branded as a legalistic misinter-
pretation of the grace of God, the purpose of
which, we fondly suppose, is to spare us the
necessity of this very breach. The saying of
Christ about hating our immediate relationships is thus turned into a cheerful affirmation of the 'God-given realities of this
world'. Once again the justification of the
sinner has become the justification of sin.[74]

This condemning of "direct" and "immediate" relationships
with the things of this world contrasts starkly with the encouragement to enjoy the good things of the earth for their own sake as
documented in the Letters and Papers from Prison. Whether there is
a contradiction here is a difficult question. Admittedly, in the
Letters, the "direct" relationship of the Christian to the things of the
earth is only made possible by the cantus firmus, or one's love for
God. In this sense, a believer can never be said to enjoy a completely
direct relationship with the good things of the earth. In this work,
nevertheless, Bonhoeffer does praise a relative independence from
Christ and His purposes, a contrapuntal dimension of human life,
and he did not do this before 1939.

The call, then, in The Cost of Discipleship, is for withdrawal
from an immediate relationship with the world. Love of God and a
love of the earth for its own sake cannot co-exist in the Christian.

Believers are instructed to live in the world, but to do so as "strangers and aliens in a foreign land", aligning themselves devoutly with the Church as the isolated community of Christ.[75] This means that the Christian must be ever aware of the breach effected by Christ between the world and Himself. Any attempt on the part of the believer to love the world on its own terms, rather than for the sake of Christ, represents a failure of faith:

> Why should we not be happy children of the
> world just because we are the children of God?
> After all, do we not rejoice in his good gifts,
> and do we not receive our treasures as a
> blessing from him? No, God and the world, God
> and its goods are incompatible, because the
> world and its goods make a bid for our hearts,
> and only when they have won them do they
> become what they really are. That is how they
> thrive, and that is why they are incompatible
> with allegiance to God. Our hearts have room
> for only one all-embracing devotion, and we
> can only cleave to one Lord.... As Jesus says,
> there is no alternative -- either we love God
> or we hate him. We are confronted by an
> 'either-or': either we love God, or we love
> earthly goods. If we love God, we hate the
> world; and if we love the world, we hate God.[76]

Christian love of God and desires for the good things of the earth for their own sake have nothing in common. In The Cost of Discipleship, Bonhoeffer speaks the "no" to earthly life which he continues to speak after 1939. But he does not yet speak the "yes" which becomes central in in the later writings. In contrast to the polyphony described in the Letters, Bonhoeffer here describes a single melody without counterpoints. In The Cost of Discipleship, Bonhoeffer does not encourage secular, contrapuntal themes, such as personal longings. Instead, purely human, earthly desires are described as competing melodies, orchestrated by Satan, and jarringly disharmonious with the Christian's love of God.

In summary, then, we do not see Bonhoeffer before 1939 urging and encouraging Christians to desire the good things of the earth for their own sake. Purely human, secular longings are acknowledged, tolerated and even recognized to be of some use in the larger purposes of God, but they are never extolled or encouraged for themselves. But now in the Letters and Papers from Prison we see him specifically affirm the intrinsic value of such desires. The

24

cantus firmus, or the believer's love of God, asists in the mastering of these desires, enabling desires to develop fully, wholly, and to their limits, even when the yearnings are not fulfilled. The love of God both promotes and sustains human desires even though they arise from our original rejection of God and seek the things of the earth for their own sake.

[1] Dietrich Bonhoeffer, Letters and Papers from Prison (enlarged edition, New York: Macmillan Paperback, 1972), pp. 271, 272.

[2] Ibid., pp. 105, 386. Bonhoeffer explains: "...in the long run, human relationships are the most important thing in life; the modern 'efficient' man can do nothing to change this... I mean...that people are more important than anything else in life. That certainly doesn't mean undervaluing the world of things and practical efficiency. But what is the finest book, or picture, or house, or estate, to me, compared to my wife, my parents, or my friend? One can, of course, speak like that only if one has found others in one's life... We must be very glad that this experience has been amply bestowed on us in our lives..."

[3] The text of "Who Am I?" is found on pages 347, 348 in the Letters, "The Past" is on pages 320, 321. In a letter to his parents on May 15, 1943 (p. 39), Bonhoeffer described his early impressions of prison life. Having been in prison for only a month, the full weight of the tension he was to experience had not yet been felt. But already he had inklings of the difficulties produced by prison life: "I'm sure I never realized as clearly as I do here what the Bible and Luther mean by 'temptation.' Quite suddenly, and for no apparent physical or psychological reason, the peace and composure that were supporting one are jarred, and the heart becomes, in Jeremiah's expressive phrase, 'deceitful above all things, and desperately corrupt; who can understand it?' It feels like an invasion from outside, as if by evil powers trying to rob one of what is most vital. But no doubt these experiences are good and necessary, as they teach one to understand life better". It was Bonhoeffer's recurring confrontation with these tensions and temptations which led him to devote such careful attention to the matter of human longings.

[4] Ibid., pp. 29, 167, 176-177, 191-192.

[5] Ibid., p. 303.

[6] Ibid., p. 41. In similar tone, Bonhoeffer adds on page 42, "Do not confound your love for one another with God". Bonhoeffer is speaking here of earthly, human, or secular desires. Henceforward, when we speak of "secular", earthly or human, we refer to things discernible in themselves, without their relationship to God being discerned.

[7]Ibid., p. 42.

[8]Ibid., pp. 191, 192 and 302.

[9]Ibid., p. 302.

[10]Ibid., pp. 168, 169.

[11]Ibid., p. 388.  For a fuller account of Bonhoeffer's view of friendship, see his poem, "The Friend" on pages 388-390.

[12]Ibid., p. 193.

[13]Ibid., p. 388.

[14]Ibid., pp. 388ff.

[15]Ibid., p. 193.

[16]Ibid., pp. 246, 247.

[17]Ibid., p. 193.  Bonhoeffer's agreement with Kierkegaard is significant.  Kierkegaard's "knight of faith" (see Fear and Trembling and Sickness Unto Death, Princeton University Press, 1970, pp. 49-50) renounces all in the act of faith, yet in that very act he paradoxically receives all back.  All the beauties and pleasures of life which he has willingly given up are returned to him to be enjoyed as never before (pp. 50, 51).  Faith is the "highest passion" for Kierkegaard (p. 43), a designation very much like Bonhoeffer's cantus firmus, or desire for God.

[18]Ibid., pp. 347, 348.  The full text of "Who Am I?" expresses Bonhoeffer's tension as he wrestled with his own desires.  To others he appeared serene and controlled, but within he often felt the profound emptiness of his loneliness.

[19]Ibid., pp. 320, 321.

[20]Ibid., p. 191.

[21]Ibid., p. 233.

[22]Ibid., p. 312.

[23]Ibid., p. 271.

[24]Ibid., p. 272.

[25]Ibid., pp. 233, 234.

[26]Ibid., pp. 233, 234.

[27]Ibid., p. 168.

[28]Ibid., p. 176.

[29]Ibid., see pages 168, 169, 191, 192, 246, and 247.

[30]Ibid., p. 167.

[31]Ibid., p. 167.

[32]Ibid., pp. 176, 1877. Bonhoeffer explains Gods role in the process of facing one's longings: "... nothing can make up for the absence of someone whom we love, and it would be wrong to try to find a substitute; we must simply hold out and see it through. That sounds very hard at first, but at the same time it is a great consolation, for the gap, as long as it remains unfilled, preserves the bonds between us. It is nonsense to say that God fills the gap; he doesn't fill it, but on the contrary, he keeps it empty and so helps us to keep alive our former communion with each other, even at the cost of pain."

[33]Ibid., p. 167.

[34]Ibid., p. 302.

[35]Ibid., p. 272.

[36]Ibid., pp. 233, 234.

[37]Ibid., p. 233.

[38]Ibid., pp. 167. 168.

[39]Ibid., p. 271.

[40]Ibid., p. 303.

[41]Ibid., p. 167.

[42]Ibid., pp. 233, 234.

[43]Ibid., p. 310.

[44]Ibid., p. 311.

[45]For an excellent explanation of the significance of the musical expression cantus firmus, see Walter Kemp's "The Polyphony of Life" in Vita Laudanda: Essays in Honor of Ulrich S. Leupold, ed. by Erich R. W. Schultz (Waterloo, Ontario, Canada: Wilfrid Laurier University Press, 1976), pp. 137-154. Kemp writes: "Bonhoeffer urges his friend to rely on the cantus firmus. One category of polyphonic composition becomes the object of the analogy, a category whose technical evolution guided the course of ecclesiastical music from the beginnings of polyphony to the seventeenth century. An already existing plainsong or secular tune... was taken as, literally, a 'fixed melody', and over it were added free contrapuntal voices... During its history the cantus firmus was subject to different treatments -- melodic ornamentation and rhythmic variation, manipulation of note values, migration of the melody to the upper voice, and permeation of the melody through all the voices. Bonhoeffer was thinking of the basic method: the cantus firmus appearing in long note values in the tenor voice, and so quite distinct from the voices in counterpoint to it... Removal of the cantus firmus voice would inflict upon the contrapuntal voices not a loss of identity as musical lines in their own merit but, more damaging, a loss of direction and purpose; as polyphonic art the composition would be invalid. The cantus firmus wills the composition and is itself the means whereby the life of that composition may rightly and successfully be enacted. This is the musical parallel to Bonhoeffer's paradox. Our faith binds to itself the varied independent strands at play in our life; it is the same faith without which no such cohesive multi-dimensional existence could have been possible for us" (pp. 145, 146). While he does not discuss the subject of our inquiry, Kemp's analysis of the cantus firmus is particularly helpful in clarifying the manner in which contrapuntal, secular themes can be relatively independent of one's love of God, and yet ultimately reliant upon it.

[46]Letters, p. 303.

[47]Ibid., p. 303.

[48]Ibid., pp. 310, 311.

[49]Ibid., pp. 302, 303.

[50]Bonhoeffer's reasons for making this assertions in the letter are not clear. He writes of the cantus firmus because he had sensed a tension in Bethge during his visit the day before. While he does not explain the nature of the stress, he apparently discerns in Bethge a tendency which Bonhoeffer fought in himself, an urge to give up, to despair of the painful longing for the one he loved. For Bonhoeffer, the temptation would have been to repress all thoughts of Maria or to seek substitutes in pious thoughts or more immediate diversions; for Bethge, the escape would have meant adopting the all-or-nothing attitude of his commanding officer toward the war effort, a readiness to fall to the last man as though nothing else in life mattered. Bonhoeffer urges his friend to rely upon his love of God to live the multi-dimensionality of his life, with its military and personal commitments, its joys and its sufferings. He counsels Bethge to live within all the dimensions of his life at once, absolutizing none at the expense of the others. Only in this way can Bethge enjoy the full riches of life. He must rest upon his love for God to find there the strength to trust in earthly life and to remain confident that all will go well.

[51]Ibid., p. 303. Before 1939, the independence of secular desires from God and His purposes was precisely the quality for which they were condemned. They were totally for themselves, hence fallen and at enmity with God. In the Letters, they remain fallen and relatively independent of God, and yet willed by Him and empowered by faith to become more fully their "independent" selves, valuable to both God and man.

[52]Ibid., p. 303.

[53]Ibid., p. 303. Bonhoeffer closes his letter to Bethge with these words: "Perhaps a good deal will be easier to bear in these days together, and possibly also in the days ahead when you're separated. Please, Eberhard, do not fear and hate the separation, if it should come again with all its dangers, but rely on the cantus firmus."

[54]See above, footnote 6.

[55]Ibid., pp. 41, 42.

[56]Dietrich Bonhoeffer, Communion of Saints (New York: Harper & Row, 1963), p. 120.

[57]Ibid., p. 131.

[58]Ibid., p. 120.

[59]Dietrich Bonhoeffer, Creation and Fall (London: SCM Press Ltd., 1959), p. 62.

[60]Ibid., p. 62.

[61]In her article, "A Query to Daniel Sullivan: Bonhoeffer on Sexuality" Continuum: Volume 4, No. 3, (Autumn 1966), pp. 457-460, Rosemary Ruether discusses the loss of man's "authentic creational being" and the loss, as well, of the paradigmatic creational community. The Fall, as she interprets Bonhoeffer, means the destruction of community, and the origin of dividedness. It is only through Christ that genuine community is restored and the I-It relation replaced with the original I-Thou relation: "Only in Christ is man recreated as communion, as the church, and only from this perspective does he dare to see his actual relationship with his created other as communion". Ruether's accurate account of the Bonhoeffer of Creation and Fall highlights a question which is central to our inquiry, namely, what is the value in the sexual desire of lovers for one another that Bonhoeffer encourages after 1939, a desire which is not mediated by Christ, but persists for its own sake?

[62]Creation and Fall, p. 79.

[63]Ibid., pp. 79, 80.

[64]Ibid., pp. 79, 80.

[65]Ibid., p. 91.

[66]Dietrich Bonhoeffer, Life Together (New York: Harper & Row, 1954), p. 31.

[67]Ibid., pp. 32, 33.

[68]Ibid., pp. 32, 33.

[69]Ibid., pp. 33, 34.

[70]Ibid., p. 38.

[71]Dietrich Bonhoeffer, The Cost of Discipleship (New York: Macmillan Paperback, 1968), p. 196.

[72]Ibid., pp. 106, 107.

[73]Ibid., pp. 314, 329.

[74]Ibid., pp. 109, 110.

[75]Bonhoeffer describes the status of the Christian in the world as follows: "God has prepared himself a people which has been justified from sin. This people is the community of the disciples of Jesus, the community of the saints. They are taken up into his sanctuary, and in fact they are his sanctuary, his temple. They are taken out of the world and live in a new realm of their own in the midst of the world... The community of the saints is barred off from the world by an unbreakable seal, awaiting its ultimate deliverance. Like a sealed train travelling through foreign territory, the Church goes on its way through the world". The Cost of Discipleship, pp. 311, 313.

[76]Ibid., p. 196. In Christian Scripture and tradition, "world" is generally defined as evil, where "earth" is defined less unequivocally. In this passage, however, it appears that Bonhoeffer's reference to "things of the world" can be equated with "things of the earth" as we have used the expression. The passage therefore stands as a sharp departure from the cited portions of the Letters which extol and encourage desires for earthly realities.

CHAPTER II
EARTHLY DESIRES IN THE LIFE OF BONHOEFFER:
BIOGRAPHICAL BACKGROUND OF THE PROBLEM

In this chapter, we intend to call attention to the correspondence between the Bonhoeffer biography and the subject of our
inquiry, namely, his urging and encouraging of personal longings.
We will rely heavily upon the efforts of Eberhard Bethge for our
biographical and historical data, but will add to his work by examining it through the lens of human, earthly desires. We will argue
that there is a personal development undergirding Bonhoeffer's positive assessment of earthly life and secular desires, a psychological
turning-point after which he praises and encourages personal
longings in a way not found in his work before 1939. We believe that
this development corresponds with and adds to the claim of a
turning-point regarding ego assertion as argued by Clifford Green.
It also corresponds with Bonhoeffer's commitment to the world, as
chronicled by Bethge. The disparity which we saw in our Chapter I
between Bonhoeffer's account of personal longings in the prison
writings with his pre-1939 corpus supports the interpretation of
Bonhoeffer's personal development which we urge in this chapter.

Bonhoeffer's concern in the 1940-1945 writings about the
experience of secular desires for other persons and for the good
things of the earth did not simply continue his previous personal
history, but reflects a vital break with the man he had been.[1] Before
1939, Bonhoeffer was preoccupied with duties, the achievement of
goals, and academic, theological and religious tasks. In addition,
Bonhoeffer lacked few of the finer things in life, and enjoyed the
security of the support and love of close friends and family. As a
result of his intellectual preoccupations, his lack of want, and a delay
in his psychological development,[2] the experience of strong
yearnings for earthly goods and for other persons was virtually
unknown to Bonhoeffer, and certainly not a central concern. At least
Bonhoeffer himself believed it to be so. In describing his past, he
recalled that he "lived many, many years...without personal longings" and "perhaps became old thereby before my time".[3]

The recollections of many who knew him lend credence to
Bonhoeffer's self-anaylsis.[4] They depict him as possessed of great
energy and vitality, and yet a man much in control of himself, his
passions, and his circumstances. His demeanor was formal and, at
times, even stern; he rarely employed the familiar "Du" form in
addressing others, even those he knew well. He insisted upon standards of excellence and intellectual precision, and rarely accepted
less from those around him. Like his father, Bonhoeffer was
impatient with shoddy thinking, and quickly rebuked his colleagues
when they expressed ill-formed opinions. His bearing was
aristocratic, his presence commanding. In short, he was a formid-

able figure. As a result, many who were physically close to him at work or play often felt at a distance from the man himself. Eberhard Bethge, his closest friend, attributes this sense of "distance", in part, to Bonhoeffer's sensitivity:

> Just as he never hurt another's feelings, he never let anyone hurt his. This made people think he was haughty. His very manner expressed this clearly. If he was angry, he expressed it in a voice that became softer, not louder. In his family, anger was not thought wrong, only indolence. They had a marked sense of the right priorities, but they possessed the quality, ascribed to many Englishmen, of treating the daily routine of life very seriously, whereas the really disturbing things, when everything was at stake, were treated as if they were quite ordinary. The stronger the emotions ran the more necessary it was to dress them in insignificant words and gestures.[5]

As Bethge suggests, Bonhoeffer held a tight rein on his emotions. Powerful emotions, in particular, were restrained by self-control and discipline. Bonhoeffer was apparently self-contained, and removed himself from the tension and risks which accompany human desiring. This reserved quality contrasts sharply with Bonhoeffer's later sustained attempts to express and feel his longings fully. As we saw in Chapter I, he wrote from prison that refusing to feel fully deprived one of experiential riches. Feeling the pain and tension of personal longings was humanly valuable. The description of Bonhoeffer offered by some of his acquaintances and this brief statement by Bethge indicate that Bonhoeffer had not always permitted himself to feel deep longings for others.

Still, Bonhoeffer exuded an assuring aura of warmth, and there were moments when a different side of the man was visible through his usual reserve which suggested the power of the rarely-observed passions beneath the surface. Johannes Goebel, for example, recounts a fascinating tale of Bonhoeffer sitting down to play the piano at Finkenwalde in 1935. Bonhoeffer, it seems, was improvising, when Goebel asked if he had ever attempted at compose anything. As Goebel tells it,

In a distinctly reserved tone he said he had

stopped doing so since he became a theologian, or something to that effect. This seems to me a typical trait of his nature. Bonhoeffer was a passionate preacher and theologian, as Bethge confirms. To sit down at an instrument and improvise or even compose... - this can only be done in passion, and out of passion. Bonhoeffer cast this passion out of his life for the sake of the call to a greater "passion".[6]

Perhaps even more suggestive than Goebel's recollection of the verbal exchange is the visual impression he received from the incident. What he remembers "seeing" is even more vivid in his memory than what he heard:

That it was a "casting out" is quite clear to me from a picture which rises in my memory, very distinctly, lit up as if by lightning, a scene which cannot be forgotten: while he was sitting at the piano something which I had not known in him and have never seen again, an expression of natural force, of something primeval, came over him, a Dietrich different from the one known to us. It was not just his natural freshness, his energy, his will-power... I do not, unfortunately, remember the musical style of his improvisation, probably because it fascinated me more to witness the native human quality breaking through his personality, than to pay attention to his music. And suddenly he stopped as abruptly as he has begun.

It is strange that this should have been so preserved by my memory; this lightening up of a rudimentary, "non-Bonhoeffer", and after that the short, harsh, sharp overcoming of himself in the way he broke off his playing so suddenly in his answer to my amiably condescending question implying such a subtle criticism of my curiosity, in the vigorous turning back to the "work", to the "essential Bonhoeffer". I can only interpret all this as an overcoming of self which, in principle, had been accomplished long before.[7]

The "natural force, of something primeval" and the "native human

36

quality" observed by Goebel were elementally human qualities suppressed by Bonhoeffer, and only occasionally seen in the man until after 1939.

We argue, as Goebel suggests, that Bonhoeffer deliberately repressed any passion for the things of the earth, his "natural", "primeval", "rudimentary" desires, in exchange for the passion of discipleship. As we saw in our Chapter I, this "overcoming of self" is a recurring theme in Bonhoeffer's writings from 1932-1939, as is the insistence upon the dualism of the world and the things of the spirit. In any case, after that time, beginning with his wrenching decision to return home from New York, Bonhoeffer lived a much more passionate life, both freeing and exercising his own vital nature. As we saw in the Letters, and will see in the biographical witness which follows, there is clearly a self-development of the sort illuminated by Goebel's recollection.

This interpretation coincides with Eberhard Bethge's description of the stages through which he observed Bonhoeffer pass.[8] Bethge marks the first turning point in Bonhoeffer's life about 1931-1932: Bonhoeffer the theologian became a Christian. According to Clifford Green, Bonhoeffer experienced a "late adolescent crisis" in the summer of 1932 and decisively rejected the "intellectual" Christianity of his past. He argues that Bonhoeffer came to view his powerful ego and his reliance upon his "(k)nowledge, education, intellectual acuteness, strength and confidence of will, creativity, mastery" as asserting himself against God and preventing a genuine life of faith and obedience.[9] As a result, he devoted himself to Christian piety, giving himself over to regular prayer, Bible study and worship. His own ambition and commitment to personal excellence, however, were still in conflict with the humility and submissiveness he now believed fundamental to Christian life. As Green explains, Bonhoeffer would not find the self-affirmation he sought in this "ego-repressive" style of Christian obedience.[10] Bethge's and Green's evidence convinces us, and we take it as a sound indication of Bonhoeffer's life-context for the intellectual development this study will argue for. But our argument does not depend upon it.

The outcome of this turning point was a committed, disciplined life in the Church, a life "quite unfamiliar to his family and to his theological teachers."[11] A letter of Bonhoeffer written in the winter of 1935-1936 seems to refer to a period in 1931 when he came to grips with the seriousness of the Christian faith:

I hurled myself into my work in an unchristian
and unhumble manner... an...ambition (Ehrgeiz)
that many noticed in me made my life difficult... Then something else came along, something which has permanently changed my life
and its direction... I had often preached, I had
seen a lot of the church, I had talked and
written about it, but I had not yet become a
Christian. (I know that until then I had been
using the cause of Jesus Christ to my own
advantage...) I had never, nor hardly ever
prayed. Despite all my abandonment, I was
very pleased (ganz froh) with myself.

The Bible, most particularly the Sermon on the
Mount, has freed me from all this. Since then
everything has changed... It was a great liber-
ation (Befreiung)... I now realized that the
life of a servant of Jesus Christ must belong
to the church, and step by step it became
clearer to me to what extend this must be so.[12]

This turning-point emerged out of Bonhoeffer's recognition
that self-aggrandizement and ambition had motivated his previous
theological work. Until that time, he passionately sought personal
success, achievement and his own advancement. In 1935, Bonhoeffer had written to his agnostic brother, Karl-Friedrich, and explained this dramatic reversal in his spiritual life. Though his
brother may regard him as "fanatical" and prefer that he be "more
reasonable", Bonhoeffer wrote that he had experienced a turnabout
in his life. For the first time, he was taking seriously the demands of
the Sermon on the Mount. Theology had become a personal matter,
calling him to "uncompromising obedience". No longer did he regard theology as an "academic affair".[13]

In another letter to his brother-in-law, Rudiger Schleicher, in
April of 1936, Bonhoeffer wrote the following:

Is it... intelligible to you if I say I am not at
any point willing to sacrifice the Bible as this
strange word of God, that on the contrary, I
ask with all my strength what God is trying to
say to us through it? Everything outside the
Bible has grown too uncertain to me. I am
afraid of running only into a divine counterpart
of myself.

38

Also I want to say to you quite personally that
since I have learned to read the Bible in this
way... it becomes more marvelous to me every
day.[14]

Bonhoeffer thus strove to reject his own powerful ego, and give himself humbly over to God's cause in Jesus Christ. As Bonhoeffer viewed his sin, it reflected Adam's. He usurped power rightfully belonging to God and sought in pride an ever-widening sphere of influence. He had sought achievement and self-satisfaction in life, but he determined to do so no more. This personal recognition brought about a "momentous change"[15] in Bonhoeffer in both his personal life and his theology.

As Bethge states, Bonhoeffer's family had nurtured its members to excel at their varied pursuits. From his early childhood Bonhoeffer possessed "an elemental drive to independence",[16] such that "his life was governed by a craving for an invariable self-real-ization".[17] Young Bonhoeffer's talents were encouraged, his strengths applauded, his achievements expected. Bonhoeffer's very decision to study theology was tainted by his wish to gain the attention of others, even to "reform" the Church where weaker men had failed.[18] Bonhoeffer did not view himself in those days as principally a servant of the Church, but more as a gift to it. But now he felt that his self-assertive style pitted him against God. He saw his drive to self-realization as a rebellious egoism, bent on replacing God with an overblown self. For his entire life he had relegated his Lord to the subordinate role of endorsing his programs and accomplishments; abruptly, he determined that the roles must be reversed, and that he must humbly serve his God in the Church.

People who had known him before this turnabout noticed the difference in him at once. His behavior was sharply altered. He began to go regularly to church, where formerly he had been rather cavalier on the matter. He undertook systematic and rigorous meditation upon the Scriptures. For the first time, he spoke seriously of oral confession as an act to be practiced and not merely discussed, a suggestion which came as more than a mild shock to his Lutheran colleagues. He talked more and more of a community of prayer and meditation, devoted to the Scriptures and the deepening of Christian fellowship.[19] While his sudden pietism disquieted some of his friends, those who knew him best found it genuine.

In addition to rejecting the power of his own ego, Bonhoeffer at the same time adopted an ascetic attitude toward earthly life. Rather unexpectedly, he put aside the pleasures of the earth as well, denying himself in another sense. The rejection of his ego reflected Bonhoeffer's confession of excessive pride and desire to become a faithful servant of Jesus Christ. His further rejection of earthly pleasures, however, did not logically or necessarily follow from the resolution of his ego problem. Perhaps Bonhoeffer linked the two in some sense, although he does not say so explicitly. For our purposes, it is significant that Bonhoeffer's first turning point produced both a denial of personal ambition and the denial of earthly joys through the adoption of a ascetic style of life.

In his letter to his brother Karl-Friedrich in January of 1935, Bon- hoeffer described his new perspective on Christian life:

> The restoration of the Church must surely come from a new kind of monasticism, which will have only one thing in common with the old, a life lived without compromise according to the Sermon on the Mount in the following of Jesus. I believe the time has come to gather people together for this.[20]

Later in that same year, Bonhoeffer was asked to direct a seminary of the Confessing Church at Finkenwalde, and there put his thoughts into practice.

The seminary community lived in an old home and had little money to make necessary repairs. As a result, they labored long hours together to render the quarters livable. The seminary routine established by Bonhoeffer was a grueling one. It consisted in prayer, meditation, and rigorous theological study. Bonhoeffer insisted upon uncompromising devotion to the community and to spiritual discipline. Yet, as reverent and serious as the seminary was, Bonhoeffer envisioned a community with an even more ascetic requirement. On September 6, 1935, he wrote to his superiors about his idea:

> With a number of students, whose names are listed below, I have proposed the plan upon which I have been ruminating for some years of setting up a Protestant Community of Brothers, in which we will, as pastors, attempt for some years to live a common Christian life.[21]

According to Bonhoeffer's proposal, the brothers would renounce all financial and other privileges which were theirs as pastors, and would serve wherever they were needed. They would take their meals and lodging at Finkenwalde, but serve without fee during the day. By the end of the month, the select brotherhood had been established. It was in this atmosphere of strict physical, mental and spiritual discipline that Bonhoeffer, his seminary students, and the working pastors of the newly-formed Bruderhaus lived until November of 1937.

These radical changes in Bonhoeffer's way of life correspond to developments in his thought. As we saw in Chapter I, in works written during the period 1932-1939, Creation and Fall (1934), The Cost of Discipleship (1937) and Life Together (1939), he sounds consistently the call to dismiss from one's life those elements which impede genuine discipleship, and to remain faithful in the midst of a fallen and condemned world. In these works he rejects the "strong" self for what Clifford Green has called the "mighty power of Christ",[22] and separates cleanly the expectations of the world from the expectations of God. Nowhere in his entire corpus is Bonhoeffer as harsh in his treatment of the world as he is in these works. Having thought too much of himself in the past, or as Clifford Green puts it, having experienced "the problem of the power of the ego in his theology and his own personal life",[23] Bonhoeffer resolved to humble himself before God, and also denied himself the things of the earth. This personal commitment is reflected in Bonhoeffer's portrayal of the things of the earth in Creation and Fall, The Cost of Discipleship and Life Together as temptations to self-interest, pleasure and forgetfulness of God.

It is little wonder, then, that during this period Bonhoeffer devoted himself to the upbuilding of the Church, and sought to dismiss from his life any egocentricity which would diminish his service to Christ. His "casting out" of earthly attachments also expressed his understanding of the selfless Christian life. It is not unreasonable to surmise that the sort of "overcoming of self", which Goebel observed, exemplified Bonhoeffer's conscious effort to put away from himself desires which he interpreted as concessions to the world and the flesh.

In 1939, however, Bonhoeffer took a major turn away from this perspective and way of life. The "second great turning point",[24] as Bethge calls it, was the transition of Bonhoeffer out of the Church and into the world, an "ambiguous world where expedients, tactics and camouflage, success and failure, all had to be carefully calculated".[25] Less reliant upon the relative security of vocation and the relative certainty attached to the Scripture and the Church, Bonhoeffer's course was now his own. He was left to trust himself, the grace of God, and the world. This "turning-point", unlike the first, can be dated rather precisely. Bethge places the date on the hot evening of June 19, 1939, when Bonhoeffer walked alone, pondering his future and the future of his nation. The decision he made, and the factors at work in its making were crucial to the subsequent course of his life and thought.

Bonhoeffer's choice in the summer of 1939 can only be appreciated when viewed in the context of the years preceding and leading to 1939. By 1939, the pressure from the Nazi authorities upon both the Confessing Church and Bonhoeffer himself had become intense. The year 1937 had seen the official closing of the preachers' seminary in Finkenwalde for "their long-standing practice of training and examining through their own organizations young theologians in defiance of the institutions set up by the State".[26] Despite legal maneuvers, petitions, and personal letters in support of the seminary, it became clear that there would be no official review of the matter. As a result, in November of 1937, their lease was terminated and the seminary disbanded.

This placed Bonhoeffer and his colleagues in the unenviable position of having to choose between operating another seminary in open defiance of the authorities,[27] running a covert educational system, or dispensing altogether with their plans for the training of pastors. It was decided that the work should continue, but under the guise of "collective pastorates".[28] This meant that young ordinands were to be installed as "learning ministers" under the administrative guidance of a senior pastor to whom they would be accountable. These "learning ministries" had been permitted by the authorities, and afforded the opportunity for the ordinands to meet together regularly for "continuing education", a euphemism for seminary training. Bonhoeffer could thus carry out his educational ministry, and continue his ascetic way of life, under far more primitive conditions, from 1938-1940. Bethge describes the arrangements in Further Pomerania as follows:

> Work and meditation, prayer, instruction in
> preaching and examination of the ideas under-
> lying the New Testament -- all this was
> carried on in the small undistracted circle
> of the collective pastorates almost more
> intensively than in the spacious house at
> Finkenwalde so close to the big town of

Stettin.[29]

The collective pastorate was personally rewarding to Bonhoeffer, but kept him extremely busy. During this time, Bonhoeffer's own life was unsettled. As Bethge points out, from the time of his collective pastorates until his death, Bonhoeffer never had a permanent residence. This was a great personal and scholarly sacrifice for Bonhoeffer, and the lack of stability made him restless. Perhaps for the first time, Bonhoeffer lacked the comforts, advantages and good things of life to which he had been accustomed. He missed the pleasure they afforded, and often wished for a better life. He often longed for a return to academia and for a more settled life, yearnings which he expressed in the following two letters:

> The only strange thing is this existence in which there can be no anxieties, because each day is a gift. If one forgets that, one sometimes gets rather restive, and would prefer to choose a more settled existence with all the "rights" that normally go with one's "rank" and one's age. That would mean abandoning the work, and it will not do at the moment.[30]

> My work goes on normally. Only one sometimes gets a bit fed up with the nomadic life, and would like to be more settled and domesticated... But it will not do just now, and I am glad to be allowed to work here.[31]

These letters show Bonhoeffer wishing to be settled down and to enjoy the rights of rank and age which were specifically renounced in the Bruderhaus at Finkenwalde. They suggest, perhaps, the beginning of a recognition that life is emptier, less fulfilling, in the absence of life's good things. The discomfiture expressed here is mild, more incovenient than debilitating, and Bonhoeffer is able to pass it off and proceed with his work. But later, the experience of deprivation returned in New York City, and again, with devastating force, in prison, and Bonhoeffer had to confront it personally and theologically.

While immersed in the work of his collective pastorates, Bonhoeffer saw the situation in Germany grow progressively worse. By 1938, a wide variety of prohibitions, restrictions, banishments and expulsions curtailed communication between members of the Confessing Church.[32] Bonhoeffer himself was placed under the "Prohibition on Entry" in January of 1938.[33] Although an appeal by his father led to his being permitted to visit home, Bonhoeffer was prevented from attending any conference in Berlin on matters of church and politics.

During the same year, an order was issued by the German Evangelical Church to the effect that all pastors were to take an oath of loyalty to the Fuhrer.[34] Despite the strenuous objections of Bonhoeffer and others, a large majority of pastors in the Confessing Church took the oath and produced a bitter division within its ranks. The eroding unity in the Confessing Church raised doubt in the minds of Bonhoeffer's seminary students over their vocational choice. Bonhoeffer struggled constantly to rally the young pastors in his circle, to convince them that their cause was just and worthy of their endurance. Many became discouraged, and conveyed to Bonhoeffer their feeling that the path of resistance had come, finally, to an end.[35]

This was a particularly painful development for Bonhoeffer, for it forced him to question the value of the work to which he was devoted. More than ever, he felt his isolation, both from his fellow theologians and from his brethren in the Confessing Church. Living under this considerable professional and personal pressure, Bonhoeffer watched as the voice of the Confessing Church grew still, the mood of anti-Semitism grew even uglier,[36] and the Germany military prepare for the imminent invasion of Czechoslovakia. It all presented a dark picture for the future of his nation and for himself. During his visits home, Bonhoeffer had occasion to speak with his brother-in-law, Hans von Dohnanyi, now deeply involved in the plot against Hitler. Dohnanyi trusted Bonhoeffer and came to him for guidance; through their intimate friendship Bonhoeffer learned of the course of the resistance to Hitler and the Nazis. From this cauldron, then, of personal disappointment with the Church, restlessness, dedication to the task of continuing the struggle against the Reich, and concern over the future welfare of his country, Bonhoeffer himself slipped quietly into the network of the resistance.[37]

His decision to enter into this covert activity corresponds to a shift of his mind away from the negative portrait of the earth emphasized in <u>Creation and Fall</u>, <u>The Cost of Discipleship</u> and <u>Life Together</u> toward a willingness to affirm the world and the Christian's participation in it. This willingness to take the things of the earth seriously in themselves, and to encourage the Christian to appreciate earthly goods for their own sake are two themes which come to the forefront in Bonhoeffer's writings and personal life after 1939.

In the winter of 1938-1939, Bonhoeffer read two booklets, The German Spirit and Christianity and Protestant Sense of History, written by Theodor Litt, a noted German philosopher and pedagogue. As a part of the overall thrust of the booklets, Litt gave a powerful endorsement of the world. Bonhoeffer heartily agreed. Bonhoeffer found lacking only an inclusion of the Incarnation as the foundation for the affirmation of earthly reality. On January 22, 1939 Bonhoeffer wrote to Litt, commending him for "loyalty to the earth", and expressing his own desire to endorse, out of faith, "the present earth in its dignity, its glory, and its curse".[38]

In the same winter of 1938-1939, Bonhoeffer began to work on a meditation on Psalm 119, a psalm which revolves almost aimlessly around the theme of commandment. As part of this meditation, Bonhoeffer wrote the following:

> The earth that nourishes me has a right to my work and my strength. It is not fitting that I should despise the earth on which I have my life; I owe her faithfulness and gratitude. I must not dream away my earthly life by thoughts of heaven, and thereby evade my lot --- that I have to be a sojourner and a stranger --- and with it God's call into this world of strangers. There is a very godless home-sickness for the other world, and it will certainly not produce any home-coming. I am to be a sojourner, with everything that that involves. I am not to close my heart indifferently to earth's problems, sorrows, and joys; and I am to wait patiently for the redemption of the divine promise --- really wait, and not rob myself of it in advance by wishing and dreaming.[39]

In both this meditation and the letter to Litt, we see Bonhoeffer taking the first steps along the path from The Cost of Discipleship to the Ethics. We see him moving toward the affirmation of the earth and of desires for the things of the earth, correlative with his evolving sense of responsibility to his world. His decision to enter the resistance movement, his decision to return to Germany later that year, and the subsequent course of his authorship were all profoundly influenced by and did influence his realization that true discipleship was not confined to the Church, but called for participation in the sufferings and joys of the earth. For Bonhoeffer, theory and lived, practical experience were intertwined. As we will see in his choice to leave New York, Bonhoeffer's allegiance to the earth and his desire for "earthly life" shaped his later life and thought.

The escalating unrest in Germany and the threat of war created the likelihood that Bonhoeffer would be conscripted into military service later in 1939. His conscience would never permit him to fight for the Reich; this was clear to him. But he feared that his refusal to serve, coupled with his status as a leading churchman, would reflect badly on the Confessing Church and further harm their cause. Bonhoeffer was deeply concerned about the well-being of his friends in the Confessing Church and the harm which is refusal to serve would cause them and their work. He believed that his unwillingness to become a part of the military was justified theologically, but he felt compelled by his love for his brethren to leave Germany, if possible, rather than take a public stand on the issue of conscription. It is probably also fair to suggest that Bonhoeffer sought a greater measure of personal peace than he was permitted in his homeland. He wanted to enjoy the academic life once again with its intellectual stimulation, its comraderie and its comforts. It was for these reasons that Bonhoeffer expressed an interest in lecturing in the United States, and sent out feelers to that effect. Reinhold Niebuhr and Paul Lehmann, with whom he had been closely associated at Union Seminary during his year of study abroad in 1930-1931, were his principal contacts. They accepted Bonhoeffer's proposal and made tentative plans whereby he would conduct a series of lectures and work with German refugees in New York.

Bonhoeffer never appeared convinced that the trip to New York was the proper course to follow. He may have sensed that the very feelings for others which prompted him to leave would ultimately draw him back to his homeland. But when his call into military service came in May of 1939 he finalized the arrangements and made preparations for the journey. In a letter to Bishop Bell, dated March 25, 1939, Bonhoeffer attempted to describe his reasons for the trip:

> I am thinking of leaving Germany sometime.
> The main reason is the compulsory military
> service to which men of my age (1906) will be
> called up this year. It seems to me con-
> scientiously impossible to join in a war under
> the present circumstances. On the other hand
> the Confessional Church as such as not taken
> any definite attitude in this respect and
> probably cannot take it as things are. So I

46

should cause a tremendous damage to my
brethren if I would make a stand on this point
which will be regarded by the regime as
typical of the hostility of our Church towards
the State. Perhaps the worst thing of all is
the military oath which I should have to swear.
So I am rather puzzled in this situation, and
perhaps even more because I feel, it is really
only on Christian grounds that I find it
difficult to do military service under the
present conditions, <u>and yet</u> there <u>are</u> only very
few friends who would approve of my attitude
[emphasis is Bonhoeffer's]. In spite of much
reading and thinking concerning this matter I
have not yet made up my mind what I should do
under different circumstances. But actually as
things are I should have to do violence to my
Christian conviction, if I were to take up arms
"here and now".[40]

The trip began on June 2 at Templehof airport, but the departure was not pleasant. Bonhoeffer was filled with misgivings. Once
again, events had taken a turn for the worse for the Confessing
Church. The majority in the Church, having already acquiesced far
beyond what Bonhoeffer could accept, continued to take measures to
accommodate the State. On the 31st of May they issued a declaration
in which they listed several minor alterations necessary to insure
their subscription to the Godesberg Declaration, an odious statement
linking National Socialism to the thought of Martin Luther and the
essence of the Christian faith.[41] As the majority of the Church
engaged in further compromise, the dwindling minority was
subjected to increased persecution. On June 1, stipends were cut off
to pastors who did not hand over their collections in the manner
prescribed by the authorities.

To make matters worse for Bonhoeffer, no one had as yet filled
his place in the collective pastorate. Bonhoeffer's anxiety over this
continuing vacancy, as well as his regard for the work carried out
there are reflected in a note he left for the man who would assume
his duties: "To my successor. He will find here: 1) one of the finest
tasks in the Confessing Church". He added, "He is asked... to go out
walking with the brethren as much as possible, or to be with them in
some other way".[42] So great was Bonhoeffer's uneasiness that he
gave Bethge a copy of his will. With all of these thoughts weighing
upon him, particularly of the friends he was leaving behind, Bon-

hoeffer departed for New York.

En route, Bonhoeffer at once wrote of his loneliness and his desire for others:

> [Journal entry] My thoughts are split between yourselves and the future... Greet all the brethren; they will be at evening prayers now.

> [To Bethge] So far I am still surprised that everything has turned out like this. I am already looking forward to your coming to see me.[43]

Thus Bonhoeffer had no sooner left Germany than he began to experience the painful longing for his friends and co-workers which would plague him until his return.

The arrival and his first hours in New York served only to heighten his misgivings. Although he was greeted warmly and embraced an an answer to the prayers of his hosts, Bonhoeffer immediately discovered that there had been a misunderstanding over the nature of his work in America and the proposed duration of his stay. Bonhoeffer had wished to leave Germany for only a short time, believing that a temporary respite would provide him opportunity to collect his thoughts and assess the events at home. He never meant to remain in New York for an extended period, and perhaps unrealistically expected an appointment flexible enough to permit his return to Germany whenever he felt it necessary. His hosts, on the other hand, had been led to believe that his very life was in danger in Germany, and that he would likely remain in America for the duration of the war. As a result, they arranged a work and lecture schedule which would occupy Bonhoeffer for at least a year, probably three. In addition to lecturing at various colleges and universities, Bonhoeffer was to supervise the care of German emigrants in New York under the aegis of the "American Committee for Christian German refugees in the City of New York".[44] This latter appointment was for three years, and would have involved him in activities clearly contrary to the aims of the Reich; accepting the appointment would have precluded his return home. His letters and diary entries indicate that Bonhoeffer at once felt trapped by the arrangements. We see Bonhoeffer profoundly moved by his desire to be with his family, loved ones and, more generally, to be back home. For the first time in his life, he experienced the depth of his need for the people he had loved and perhaps taken for granted in Germany. His decision to return to Germany was made after his journal entry

of June 18, so the context of the subsequent entries is altered by that
fact. But throughout his journal, both before and after his decision,
runs the theme we see repeated and developed in the Letters and
Papers from Prison, namely, his longing for others.

> Very warm and "informal" reception --- In all
> this only Germany and the brothers are
> missing. The first lonely hours are hard. I
> cannot make out why I am here, whether it
> makes sense, whether the result will justify
> it... Nearly two weeks have passed now,
> without my hearing anything from over there.
> It is hardly to be borne. (June13, 1939)

> Since yesterday evening I can hardly tear my
> thoughts away from Germany... I found a drive
> to visit a friend in the hills, in itself de-
> lightful, almost unendurable. We sat for an
> hour and chatted, not all that stupidly, but
> about matters to which I was entirely in-
> different... and I thought how usefully I
> might have employed this hour in Germany.
> (June 15, 1939)

> There is no time to waste, and here I am
> wasting days and it may be weeks. At any
> rate, it looks like that at the moment...
> Disturbing political news from Japan. If
> things become unsettled, I shall certainly
> return to Germany. I cannot stay alone outside
> the country. That is quite clear to me. I am
> living completely over there... (June 16, 1939)

> ...Through my intention and my interior
> necessity, continually to remember the
> brothers over there and their work, I have been
> almost abandoning my task over here. It would
> seem to me almost like disloyalty if my heart
> were not completely in Germany. I must find
> the right balance in this. (June 18, 1939)

> ...Of course I still go on wondering about my
> decision... one might ask, have I acted simply
> out of longing for Germany and the work there?
> And was my almost incomprehensible and
> hitherto unknown homesickness an accom-

panying sign from above which was to make
the refusal easier? (June 21, 1939)

It is for us as it is for soldiers, who come
home on leave from the front but who, in spite
of all their expectations, long to be back at the
front again. We cannot get away from it
anymore. Not because we are necessary, or
because we are useful (to God?), but we leave
our life behind, destroy it, if we cannot be in
the midst of it again. It is nothing pious, more
like a vital urge. But God acts not only by
means of pious incentives, but also through
such vital stimuli. (June 26, 1939)

The journey is finished. I am glad to have
been here and glad to be on the way home
again. Perhaps I have learned more in this
month than in a whole year nine years ago; at
least I have realized things which will be
important for future decisions. Probably this
journey will have a prolonged effect upon me.
(July 7, 1939)[45]

These entries, which all sound a common note of longing for
the life and the persons he had left behind, mark distinct stages
through which Bonhoeffer passed as he wrestled with his decision.
A homesickness plagued him throughout his journey and his brief
stay in New York, a terrible homesickness which is "hardly to be
borne". Bonhoeffer acknowledged the power of his desires; he knew
that somehow he must confront them, understand them, and come
to grips with his yearnings in a way which resolved his inner
turmoil.

At first, we see Bonhoeffer questioning the value of coming to
New York. His first journal entries suggest an attempt to settle the
matter rationally. He asks himself, "...why I am here, whether it
makes sense, whether the result will justify it". Had Bonhoeffer
pushed these preliminary inquiries further, he would have been
forced to acknowledge that the work entrusted to him in New York
was important and potentially fulfilling.[46] His lecturing would have
provided him with the academic stimulus and the settled life for
which he had longed in Germany. By his pastoral work with
refugees he would indeed participate in the fate of his people, and
satisfy his need for continuing involvement in the ministry. Further,
it remained the case that his return would probably prove disad-

vantageous to the Confessing Church and to himself. Bonhoeffer knew these things when he left; in fact, it was for these reasons he had gone. The factors in the equation had not changed dramatically since his departure. The new factor, however, which changed everything, was his overwhelming desire to go home, echoed in each of the entries cited.

Bonhoeffer soon realized that this was so. He abandoned his search for a rational course of action. He found conversations which would ordinarily have been "delightful" to be unendurable; he regarded his assignments with indifference, as a "waste" of time: he even found himself "almost abandoning" the tasks set aside for him. This troubled Bonhoeffer deeply, for he knew the value of the work and the caliber of the people with whom he was associated. Still, he could not bring himself to face the tasks at hand. His journal and letters show him paralyzed by his feelings. He resolved to "find the right balance in this", and proceeded with an examination of his enervating homesickness.

On June 18, Bonhoeffer declared his "intention and interior necessity, continually to remember the brothers over there and their work". For the next several days he grappled with the nature and source of this "interior necessity". He wondered on June 21, two days after he decided to return, whether he acted solely on the basis of his "longing for Germany and the work there...", and pondered whether his homesickness was "an accompanying sign from above to make the refusal easier..." The question suggests a theological intuition which Bonhoeffer would later unpack at some length, namely, that secular desires are both relatively independent of God and yet ultimately dependent upon Him and serve His higher purposes.

On June 26, as he further pondered the yearnings to which he has acceded, Bonhoeffer characterized desire as an expression of the force of "life" within us. It is not something "pious", but a "vital urge" which draws us back to the midst of our own lives. In thoughts which we find later taken up in the Letters, Bonhoeffer wondered if God was acting through his natural desires. Bonhoeffer acknowledged his desires as a part of his life, to be accepted as such. This tentative conclusion enabled Bonhoeffer to face his longings and to accept them, discovering perhaps that we need moral discernment and effort to recognize desires and follow them.

> We cannot get away from it anymore. Not
> because we are necessary, or because we are
> useful (to God?), but simply because that is
> where our life is, and because we leave our

life behind, destroy it, if we cannot be in the
midst of it again.

Bonhoeffer discovered that his life was in Germany and that,
despite the challenge of his work in New York and the quality and
warmth of the people there, he "had" to return home.  His desires
were forcing him to return to his friends, to his country, and to his
life.  He knew well what such a choice would mean.  He would cause
disappointment, ill feelings, and disruptions in the work assigned to
him.  But Bonhoeffer "had" to leave.  After a long walk around Times
Square on the evening of June 19, Bonhoeffer communicated his
decision to Henry Leiper of the Federal Council of Churches the next
morning, and conveyed his regrets to Reinhold Niebuhr in letter:

> I have made a mistake in coming to America.  I
> must live through this difficult period in our
> national history with the Christian people of
> Germany.  I will have no right to participate
> in the reconstruction of Christian life in
> Germany after the war if I do not share the
> trials of the time with my people... Christians
> in Germany will face the terrible alternative
> of either willing the defeat of their nation in
> order that Christian civilization may survive,
> or willing the victory of their nation and
> thereby destroying our civilization.  I know
> which of these alternatives I must choose; but
> I cannot make that choice in my security.[47]

Bonhoeffer's choice became a clear one, for the force of his desires
tipped the scales in favor of a swift return to Germany.  His desires,
in effect, left him no choice.  They drew him to the peole he loved and
to the nation whose trials he would share.  He returned home
because he was compelled to do so by his longings for all he had left
behind and because he sensed that it was God's will that he follow
the thrust of his desires.

Although we have attributed importance to this episode in
Bonhoeffer's life, scholars are not in agreement about its significance.  In a recent study,[48] James Patrick Kelley devotes a great
deal of attention to Bonhoeffer's decision in the summer of 1939.  At
issue is the legitimacy of characterizing the visit to America as a
"personal crisis" or "major turning point" in Bonhoeffer's life and
thought.  In particular, Kelley debates the claims of David Hopper[49]
and Clifford Green[50] that Bonhoeffer's short stay in New York had a

deep impact upon his theological development as well as his self-understanding.

Hopper contends that Bonhoeffer was disoriented and confused while in New York, and that his experience led him explicitly to endorse an "aristocratic Chrisitianity", latent in his earlier thought. This turn in his theology was marked by a retreat from the "weakness theme" of his "middle period" into a theme of strength,[51] which encouraged Christians to develop their native abilities to the fullest and to reject the flight of piety in exchange for the assertive worldliness of genuine discipleship. This motif is said by Hopper to dominate the Letters and Papers from Prison, reaching its apex in the affirmation of earthly strengths and abilities without reference to the purposes of God.

Green's interpretation is more psychological in orientation, but his conclusions are similar. Green feels that Bonhoeffer underwent "a deep, existential struggle" during his visit to New York which was "...a watershed... [the] development" of a new perspective on discipleship and worldliness. With his decision to return to Germany, Bonhoeffer, for the first time, was "free to affirm his own strengths, overcoming the self-violation he had advocated earlier".[52]

Kelley takes issue with these interpretations. He maintains that Bonhoeffer sought consistently to retain "both a theology of revelation, on the one hand, and the importance and inherent validity of the most mundane and 'secular' realities in such a theology, on the other..."[53] He traces the subtle shifts in Bonhoeffer's expression of this Christological dialectic throughout the corpus, and argues that major breaks in Bonhoeffer's thought simply do not occur. Kelley therefore finds excessive the claims of Hopper and Green. Since Kelley maintains one coherent Christological dialectic from beginning to end in Bonheffer's work, he marshals considerable theological and historical evidence to refute Hopper's notion of the "personal crisis" in 1939 which produced a "major break" in Bonhoeffer's thought.

Kelley insists that the events of 1939 do not require the kind of "dramatic" portrayal given them by Hopper. In fact, he charges that the assertion of a "personal crisis" in the summer of 1939 "conveniently ignores those data which count against this simplistic picture".[54] Kelley concurs that some confusion attended Bonhoeffer's decision to return to Germany, but he attributes it to the unexpected nature and duration of the arrangements made in New York and to the worsening conditions at home. He points out that Bonhoeffer had met on several occasions with leaders of the <u>Abwehr</u> section before his departure for New York, and had reason to believe that he would be offered a civilian appointment upon his return. This would have enabled him to avoid military conscription while, at the same time, to participate in the resistance movement. The awareness of this option, should he return to Germany, added to Bonhoeffer's distress and disillusionment during the days in New York. Kelley also makes much of the misunderstandings which led to appointments far more demanding of Bonhoeffer's time than he had anticipated or wished. This, Kelley suggests, was a fundamental cause of Bonhoeffer's return. Finally, he accuses Hopper of failing to note the persistence of the "weakness theme" in portions of the <u>Ethics</u> written subsequent to the "crisis" of 1939.

With reference to Green, Kelley cautions against the tendency to read Bonhoeffer as a "psychological diagnostician" might, and argues that a careful scrutiny of the texts does not suggest a "radical conversion of style". Instead, Kelley speaks of a "development", even a "turning point" but one which possessed "the character of an extended transition emerging from various adjustments of his views to the new circumstances he faced".[55] Kelley is justified in his rejection of the notion of a "major turning point" in Bonhoeffer's theological direction in the summer of 1939, insofar as this designation would indicate a total break or radical discontinuity with his past. His arguments from the text, particularly from the <u>Ethics</u>, are convincing. But there is little doubt that the "crisis" moved Bonhoeffer toward the affirmation of the value of earthly desires and toward his praise and encouragement of personal longings, directions which he might not otherwise have taken. Kelley's debate with Green on the question of a "turning point" or "break" seems largely semantic.[56] Whether one calls the transition in Bonhoeffer's thought a turning point or a development, an important shift did clearly occur in 1939. The historical evidence and the textual evidence from his personal writings prove a crisis here. In addition, as we have seen, Bonhoeffer praises and encourages personal longings in the <u>Letters</u> in a manner which is not continuous with the pre-1939 corpus.

Kelley correct points to the possibility of an appointment to the <u>Abwehr</u>, and to Bonhoeffer's obvious dissatisfaction with the arrangements made in America, but he neglects Bonhoeffer's own letters and diary entries from the days in New York, from which such matters are virtually absent. Nowhere does Bonhoeffer mention other possibilities awaiting him in Germany, and nothing is said of the <u>Abwehr</u>. This is significant because Bonhoeffer would not have had to conceal such a possibility from German authorities, and could have written freely about his prospects had they been central in his decision-making. The fact that he omits this option from his written meditation on his dilemma strongly suggests that the Abwehr was not at the forefront of his thinking, as Kelley indicates. As our analysis of his correspondence and diary has shown, he reaches his decision on the basis of very different sorts of considerations. The more deeply Bonhoeffer ponders his circumstances, the more he realizes that his desires are the compelling factor in the equation. He no longer weighs options objectively; instead, he acknowledges that his "interior necessity" and "vital urges" leave him no alternative. The decision reached in 1939 represents a "personal crisis" for Bonhoeffer because he came to grips for the first time with the reality, importance and value of his own desires, a realization that had a "prolonged effect" upon him and decidedly affected his later writing.

Our study is concerned with Bonhoeffer's treatment of desires after 1939, for his thoughts on the subject after that time are unique to his corpus, and central to the understanding of his later theology. As we have shown thus far, Bonhoeffer never praised or encouraged secular yearnings before 1939, or before the "crisis" we discussed. In what follows, we will present the first signs of encouragement for earthly desires to be with those we love as they appear after Bonhoeffer's return to Germany. We will see Bonhoeffer beginning to write in a manner which contrasts sharply with his work before 1939, and which further supports our argument for a "crisis" in New York. In our next chapter, we will show how these occasions are a part of a theological development clearly traceable in the Ethics.

Records are scanty, but we know several occasions between the time of his return to Germany and his imprisonment in April of 1943 when Bonhoeffer affirms the value and importance of earthly desires. These occasions are his discussions with Oskar Hammelsbeck, his correspondence with Eberhard Bethge and Erwin Sutz, and his engagement to Maria von Wedemeyer. Obviously, during this time Bonhoeffer focused his energies upon the resistance movement and the plots to remove Hitler. But, as we have seen, his desire for life's good things and his willingness to take the earth seriously in itself were, in part, responsible for his commitment to the overthrow of the Reich. Bethge agrees that by participating in the resistance, Bonhoeffer moved away from the negative view of earthly life expressed in Creation and Fall, The Cost of Discipleship and Life Together. He was now willing to give himself over to service to the world, for the sake of the world, as he expressed in his letter to Niebuhr. Bethge describes the winter of 1941, a period of Bonhoeffer's deepening involvement in the underground, in the following manner:

> ...it was a grotesue situation for the man of
> The Cost of Discipleship and of the ecumenical
> movement --- a confidential agent ("V-Mann")
> in Germany's war machine... Those who com-
> missioned Bonhoeffer wanted to make him and
> his unusual foreign connections serve their
> political aims for Germany; and he no longer
> wanted to withdraw from those who were
> hazarding their own lives to achieve those
> aims. He was no longer tied to the seminary or
> to any congregation. The means were now to
> be tested on the basis of their greatest pos-
> sible fitness for the end in view, now that the
> only way that remained open was that of
> "conspiracy".[57]

"Conspiracy" for Bonhoeffer meant an expression of true Christian
worldliness for the purpose of preserving the earthly realities and the
Christian civilization he held dear. Perhaps no stronger evidence
exists for Bonhoeffer's desire for the things of the earth than his
willingness to sacrifice himself on their behalf.

Bonhoeffer expressed his appreciation for the things of the
earth in discussions with Oskar Hammelsbeck shortly after his
return from America. Hammelsbeck had devoted himself to the
Confessing Church after an active life in the secular realm, and had
assisted in the work of the collective pastorate during Bonhoeffer's
stay in New York. His ties to the world, however, remained strong,
and he was concerned that the Church retain its contact with the
secular sphere and respectfully exert its influence upon it. It was
here, Bethge explains, that Hammelsbeck "found a partner in Bonhoeffer... who was now also engaged in reuniting secular existence
and the Church".[58] Out of this shared concern, Bonhoeffer and
Ham- melsbeck met for personal discussions in the fall of 1939. An
entry in Hammelsbeck's diary from 1941 provides us with his
recollection of these meetings in 1939:

> The question whether my way into the Church
> can be directed back into the world, that wor-
> rying question about the Christian's respons-
> ibility to the world, the question "Church for
> the World", was exactly what Dietrich Bon-
> hoeffer was asking, and so the conversations
> with him were the most important also for me

56

at that period...[59]

In the meetings, Bonhoeffer disclosed his connections with the resistance movement, indicating thereby the extent of his personal commitment to the future of the earth. The discussions anticipated Bonhoeffer's later thought also, as recorded in another entry of Hammelsbeck's diary of January 1941:

> We can make no progress here till we radically grasp the idea of our "godless" existence in the world. That means, till we refuse to entertain any illusion of being able to act "with God" from day to day in the world. That illusion repeatedly misleads us into throwing away justification and grace, into artificial piety, into making a legalized ethic, and to becoming unfree in a servitude with all the signs changed...[60]

In his talks with Hammelsbeck, as in his correspondence with Theodor Litt, Bonhoeffer incorporates a love for life and for the earth into a coherent form of Christian obedience, albeit a different form from the one he advocated prior to 1939. This more positive stance toward earthly life undergirds Bonhoeffer's later affirmation of desires for the good things of the earth for their own sake.

Only a year after his return to Germany, we observe Bonhoeffer openly expressing his persistent desire for Bethge to visit him at Ettal. The five months spent by Bonhoeffer in Munich and Ettal was the first lengthy separation from Bethge during their friendship, and Bonhoeffer found it difficult to bear. He longed to see Bethge, and to share his new experiences with him. Excerpts from his letters to Bethge during this period express the demanding and dependent quality of his feelings.

> It is a beautiful winter here. I hope you will come! (Munich, October 31, 1940)
>
> Now you will be preparing for the Bible week. A pity that we cannot again prepare for it together... (Munich, November 4, 1940)
>
> How nice it would be, if we could do something together. Can you think of a solution to this?... When are you coming? (Munich, October 31, 1940)

...I am here since yesterday, received in a most
friendly manner... I only miss my writing
table, and the opportunity to share my impressions which during the last six years has
become a matter of course... I wanted also to
tell you in addition to your invitation here that
I have excellent personal contacts with the
largest Catholic Missionary Society... I wonder
whether that would not justify your journey?
(Ettal, November 18, 1940)

The inborn hospitality here, which is evidently
something specifically Benedictine, the honour
which is shown to the stranger for the love of
Christ, makes one almost ashamed. You really
ought to come here! It is an enrichment...
(Ettal, November 23, 1940)

...So I suggest that you come here immediately
after East Prussia... (Ettal, Advent I, 1940)

... In the meantime you will have read from the
20th onwards, travelling is to be made more
difficult. So we must soon make up our minds.
(Ettal, December 5, 1940)

...of course, I will meet you in Munich. (Ettal,
December 10, 1940)

Will you prefer to travel second class, a day
journey? If you take something pleasant to
read... it might actually be quite restful...
(Ettal, December 11, 1940)[61]

These letters show the power of Bonhoeffer's longing for Bethge, and
his openness in expressing it. Our accounts of Bonhoeffer's emo-
tional reserve before 1939 suggest that he could not have expressed
this kind of feeling as openly before that time, if he had had it.

Bonhoeffer affirms humanly desires, too, on his trip to
Switzerland in 1941. At that time, Bonhoeffer visited a friend, Erwin
Sutz, and congratulated him on his recent marriage. His language
is strikingly similar to that later used in his wedding sermon to Eberhard and Renate Bethge in 1943. Writing to Sutz, he commended
him on his plans for the future:

58

...now in the midst of demolition, we want to
build up; in the midst of life by the day and by
the hour, we want a future; in the midst of
banishment from the earth, a bit of room; in
the midst of the general distress, a bit of happiness. And what overwhelms us is that God
says Yes to this strange desire, that God acquiesces in our will, though the reverse should
normally be true. So marriage becomes something quite new, mighty, grand for us who want
to be Christians in Germany.[62]

Bonhoeffer approves this "strange desire" unambiguously. Man has
a right to his desires for happiness, earthly hopes, peace of mind,
and the solace of others. God Himself adds His "Yes" to man's
yearning earthly life. The desires themselves are solely secular in
nature, and yet are applauded in their own right.

The value and importance of earthly desires to Bonhoeffer is
further revealed in his courtship with Maria von Wedemeyer. From
his first meeting with Maria and her parents, Hans and Ruth von
Wedemeyer, Bonhoeffer was struck by a natural, vital quality in the
family. When Hans lost his life on the eastern front in 1942,
Bonhoeffer spoke of this impression in a letter of condolence to his
wife:

When, as the years went by, I got to know
nearly all your children, I was often impressed
by seeing what a great blessing it is to have a
truly Christian father. It is really one and the
same impression that I have felt as deeply in
meeting your family and relatives... The blessing is, indeed, not something purely spiritual,
but something that goes deep down to affect
one's earthly life. Under the real blessing, life
becomes sound, firm, confident, active, just
because it is lived from the source of life, of
strength, joy, and action.[63]

His description of life under "the real blessing" bears a faint
resemblance to his cantus firmus metaphor in the Letters. Strong
faith, in each case, promotes confidence in living earthly life. It was
this confident, earthly vitality which he had come to value which, in
part, drew Bonhoeffer to Maria. When he saw her as a young
woman, several years after her instruction for confirmation, Bon-

hoeffer was disquieted by the feelings she produced in him. In a letter to Bethge in August of 1942, he expressed his uneasiness:

> I have not written to Maria. As things stand it
> is impossible now. If no further meeting is
> possible, the delightful thought of a few min-
> utes of high tension will no doubt melt once
> again in the realm of unfulfilled fantasies that
> is already adequately populated in any case.
> On the other hand, I do not see how a meeting
> could be contrived that she would find unob-
> trusive and inoffensive. One cannot expect
> that of Frau von Kleist either, in any case not
> as an idea of mine, for I am really not at all
> clear about it yet.[64]

Bonhoeffer later used the expression "high tension" in the Letters to describe the value and riches of intense feelings. Here, in 1942, he recognizes the importance of deep feelings and speaks of their value, even if the longings shoud remain unfulfilled. Further meetings with Maria, however, convinced him that he must see more of her. Her mother, at the same time, sensed the depth of the feelings in- volved, and called upon Bonhoeffer to discuss matters with her on the 24th of November. The result of their conversation was the "sug- gestion" by Maria's mother that the two remain apart for a year, allowing her daughter time to mature and bring greater wisdom to any decisions they would later wish to make.

This development upset Bonhoeffer very much. He commun- icated his frustration in a letter to Bethge three days later:

> I think I could get my way if I wanted to; I can
> argue better than the others and could probably
> talk her round; but that would not be natural
> to me, it seems to me wrong... and like
> exploiting other people's weakness. Frau von
> Wedemeyer is stronger through the loss of her
> husband --- that is, in her very weakness ---
> than if I had had to deal with him, too. I must
> not allow her to feel defenseless; that would
> be mean, but it makes my situation more diff-
> icult.[65]

Bonhoeffer wrote several more times to Bethge, seeking his aid and counsel, but discovered, as he had in New York, that his longing could not be argued or negotiated away. Despite the reasons for waiting, including Maria's youth, her mother's understandable concern and prohibition, and Bonhoeffer's own wish to proceed properly, he abruptly became engaged to Maria von Wedemeyer on January 27, 1943.

[1]The nature of this "break" is a matter of scholarly debate. Our position in relation to the break will be discussed at a later juncture; for now, it should suffice to say that we support the view that a decisive shift in Bonhoeffer's life and thought commenced in the summer of 1939.

[2]Clifford Green, "Bonhoeffer in the Context of Erickson's Luther Study", in Psychohistory and Religion, ed. by Roger Johnson (Philadelphia: Fortress Press, 1977), p. 186.

[3]Dietrich Bonhoeffer, Letters and Papers from Prison (enlarged edition: New York: Macmillan paperback, 1972), pp. 271-272. The German in this passage (gelebt habe; ist alt geworden) usually equivelates the simple English past tense. The questionable translation "I have lived", suggests that Bonhoeffer is reviewing his life up until the date of the letter in question, April 11, 1944. The more likely translation "I lived", leaves open the question of when Bonhoeffer came to acknowledge the value of his own desires. The proper translation, therefore, does not militate against the significance of 1939 as a watershed year in Bonhoeffer's way of life.

[4]For a sense of the personality of Bonhoeffer, I Knew Dietrich Bonhoeffer (Wold-Dieter Zimmerman and Ronald Gregor Smith ed., New York: Harper and Row, 1964) is an excellent resource. References in support of the brief character sketch offered in my main text include the following: pp. 42, 43 and 45 (Paul Lehmann), pp. 62, 65 and 66 (Wolf-Dieter Zimmermann), p. 80 (Lawrence Whitburn), p. 82 (Otto Dudzus), pp. 123-125 (Johannes Goebel), pp. 126-128 (Albrecht Schonherr), pp. 132 and 134 (Wilhelm Bott) and pp. 153 and 155 (Hans-Werner Jensen).

[5]Eberhard Bethge, Dietrich Bonhoeffer: Man of Vision, Man of Courage (New York: Harper and Row, 1970), p. XXIV.

[6]I Knew Dietrich Bonhoeffer, p. 124.

[7]Ibid., pp. 124, 125.

[8]For a more thorough account of the "turning points" in Bonhoeffer's life see Eberhard Bethge, "Turning Points in Bonhoeffer's Life and Thought", Bonhoeffer in a World Come of Age, Peter Vorkink, ed. (Philadelphia: Fortress Press, 1968), pp. 73-102.

[9]Clifford Green, Bonhoeffer: The Sociality of Christ and Humanity (Missoula, Montana: Scholars Press, 1972), p. 166.

[10]Green, "Bonhoeffer in the Context of Erickson's Luther Study", p. 186.

[11]Bethge, Dietrich Bonhoeffer..., p. 153ff.

[12]Ibid., p. 54.

[13]This letter to his brother is reproduced in Bethge's Dietrich Bonhoeffer, p. 155. Dated January 14, 1935, the letter reads as follows: "It may be that in many things I may seem to you rather fanatical and crazy. I myself am sometimes afraid of this. But I know that, if I were 'more reasonable', I should in honour bound be compelled to give up the whole of my theology. When I first began, I imagined it quite otherwise --- perhaps as a more academic matter. Now something very different has come of it. I now believe that I know at last that I am at least on the right track --- for the first time in my life. And that often makes me very glad...I believe that I know that inwardly I shall be really clear and honest with myself only when I have begun to take seriously the Sermon on the Mount. That is the only source of power capable of blowing up the whole phantasmagoria once and for all... I still cannot really believe you genuinely believe all these ideas to be so completely crazy. There are things for which an uncompromising stand is worth while. And it seems to me that peace and social justice, or Christ himself, are such things". Bethge notes that the term "phantamagoria" refers to Hitler and his rule.

[14]Gesammelte Schriften, Vol. III (Munich: Kaiser, 1966), pp. 28ff. Translated by Bethge in Dietrich Bonhoeffer, pp. 155, 156.

[15]Bethge, Dietrich Bonhoeffer, p. 153.

[16]Ibid., p. 23.

[17]Ibid., p. 23.

[18]Ibid., pp. 22ff. Bethge summarizes Bonhoeffer's decision to study theology with these words: "He set out on the path to theology from an essentially worldly base. First of all, there was the 'call' that came to him in his youthful vanity to something special in life. Then intellectual curiosity plunged him into theology as a branch of knowledge. Only later did the Church come into his field of vision. Unlike

theologians who have come from church and theological families and have discovered the existence of the 'world' only later Bonhoeffer set out on his journey and eventually discovered the Church" (p. 28).

[19]Ibid., pp. 153, 154.

[20]Gesammelte Schriften, Vol. III (Munich: Kaiser, 1966), p. 25. Translated by Mary Bosanquet in The Life and Death of Dietrich Bonhoeffer (New York: Harper and Row, 1968), p. 150.

[21]Gesammelte Schriften, Vol. II (Munich: Kaiser, 1965), p. 448. Translated by Mary Bosanquet in The Life and Death of Dietrich Bonhoeffer, p.156.

[22]Green, Bonhoeffer: The Sociality of Christ and Humanity, p. 187.

[23]Ibid., p. 203.

[24]Eberhard Bethge, "Turning Points in Bonhoeffer's Life and Thought", p. 89.

[25]Ibid., p. 89.

[26]Eberhard Bethge, Dietrich Bonhoeffer, p. 490.

[27]This course had been taken by H.J. Iwand who tried to reopen his East Prussian seminary on the authority of Superintendent F. Heuner. The authority responded by arresting all involved and expelling them from Dortmund, the new site of the seminary. Other seminaries were closed as well. Bonhoeffer and his associates took careful note of this precedent and thought it more prudent to continue the work under the guise of the collective pastorate. See Dietrich Bonhoeffer, pp. 493ff.

[28]Ibid., p. 494.

[29]Ibid., p. 497.

[30]Gesammelte Schriften, Vol. I (Munich, Kaiser, 1965), pp. 48ff. Translated by Bethge in Dietrich Bonhoeffer, p. 499.

[31]This letter of December, 1938 is reproduced by Eberhard Bethge in Dietrich Bonhoeffer, p. 499.

[32]The State's effort to jam the communication lines of the Church was largely successful due to its imposition of numerous restraints and prohibitions. Bethge describes the nature and extent of these orders: "...one had to get used to a range of new expressions for 'restraints'. The headings now read: Prohibitions against Preaching, Expulsions, Banishments, Prohibitions of Exit and Entry, Ministerial Prohibitions. Every measure thus named was deliberately graded so as to make communication between the leading men of the Confessing Church impossible without their being arrested." The result was a sharp decrease in the number of arrests, but a marked increase in the level of repression. In August of 1938, Bethge reports that there were "11 ministerial prohibitions, 150 prohibitions on exit and entry, expulsions and banishments, 44 prohibitions against preaching and only 11 arrests (pp. 501, 502)".

[33]A "Prohibition of Entry" prevented important members of the Confessing Church from attending conferences and meetings in Berlin. At the same time, "Prohibitions on Exit" virtually imprisoned men like Niesel, Albertz, Bohm and F. Muller in Berlin and severed their communication with other Church leaders.

[34]The text of the oath was as follows: "I swear that I will be faithful and obedient to Adolf Hitler, the Fuhrer of the German Reich and people, that I will conscientiously observe the laws and carry out the duties of my office, so help me God". Those refusing to take the oath were to be dismissed from the ministry (Dietrich Bonhoeffer, pp. 504, 505).

[35]Two letters received by Bonhoeffer in 1939 express the dilemma imposed upon the young pastors by the times:

> "The question I ask myself is what I ought to do if actually, at any rate here in Pomerania, the Confessing Church has got to the end of the road. Should I look for another profession? Or should I say: against my better judgment and against my ecclesiastical convictions I will go to the Konsistorium because otherwise it is impossible for me to follow my vocation?"

> "I cannot regard the continuation of the course which we have followed hitherto as theologically justified or as one for which I can be responsible either in my own case or in that or others."

These letters from O. Kirstner and G. Krause respectively, are reproduced in Dietrich Bonhoeffer, pp. 514-515.

[36]During the year 1938, Jews were placed under additional restrictions, which included the stamping of the letter "J" on their passports to monitor and limit their travel.  Bonhoeffer's own sister and her husband, himself a Jew, were forced to flee the country in the face of the deteriorating conditions.  On the 9th of November, on what came to be known as "Crystal Night", a synagogue was burned in Köslin and acts of terror were carried out against the Jewish populace throughout Germany.  The muted voice of the Confessing Church had little to say about the widespread pogroms.  This further convinced Bonhoeffer that the Confessing Church and Germany itself were heading toward darker times.  See Dietrich Bonhoeffer, pp. 507, 511 and 512.

[37]The story of Bonhoeffer's gradual involvement in the resistance movement has been chronicled by Bethge and others.  It does not need repeating in detail for our purposes.  We wish to offer an historical and personal context out of which Bonhoeffer came to value earthly life and personal longings.  His growing political involvement and the individuals he met in their common cause, were to have a profound effect upon his perspectives on discipleship and Christian worldliness.

[38]Gesammelte Schriften, Vol. III (Munich:  Kaiser, 1966), pp. 31-33.  Translated by Eberhard Bethge in Dietrich Bonhoeffer, pp. 618.

[39]Gesammelte Schriften, Vol. IV (Munich:  Kaiser, 1965), p. 538.  Translated by Eberhard Bethge in Dietrich Bonhoeffer, pp. 524, 525.

[40]Gesammelte Schriften, Vol. I (Munich:  Kaiser, 1965), pp. 281ff.  Eberhard Bethge sums up Bonhoeffer's personal turmoil on the eve of his trip to New York in the following fashion: "On church matters what disturbed him most were:  the question of the oath, the efforts to achieve unity, the treatment of the young 'illegal' pastors, and the reaction to the special prayers and 'Crystal Night'.  In political matters, he was disturbed by the failure to overthrow Hitler, the preparations for war, and the supposed exclusion of Dohnanyi from the Berlin circle.  As to personal matters, we have already mentioned the restlessness of life in the collective pastorate, the imminent call-up, and his emigrant sister's fate" (Dietrich Bonhoeffer, p. 540).

[41]The Godesburg Declaration, reproduced in part by Bethge read as follows: "[National Socialism continues] the work of Martin Luther on the ideological and political side, [and this helps], in its religious aspect, the recovery of a true understanding of the Christian faith... The Christian faith is the unbridgeable religious contrast to Judaism... Supranational and international churchism of a Roman Catholic or world-Protestant character is a political degeneration of Christianity. A fruitful development of genuine Christian faith is possible only within the given orders of creation" (Dietrich Bonhoeffer, p. 549).

[42]Gesammelte Schriften, Vol. II (Munich: Kaiser, 1965), pp. 551ff. Translated by Eberhard Bethge in Dietrich Bonhoeffer, p. 553.

[43]These journal entries are reproduced in Dietrich Bonhoeffer, p. 554.

[44]Ibid., p. 556.

[45]Gesammelte Schriften, Vol. I (Munich: Kaiser, 1965), pp. 292-320. Cf, Mary Bosanquet, The Life and Death of Dietrich Bonhoeffer (New York: Harper and Row, 1968), pp. 209ff.

[46]In what follows, we are merely arguing that a strong case could have been made in favor of Bonhoeffer's remaining in New York if the decision had been reached through a form of cost/benefit analysis. The intangible factor, his longing for his loved ones and his homeland, transcended such an analysis and was the fundamental cause for his return.

[47]Gesammelte Schriften, Vol. I (Munich: Kaiser, 1965), p. 320. Translated by Bethge in Dietrich Bonhoeffer, p. 559.

[48]James Patrick Kelley, Revelation and the Secular in the Theology of Dietrich Bonhoeffer (Ann Arbor, Michigan: University Microfilms International, 1980).

[49]David Hopper, A Dissent on Bonhoeffer (Philadelphia: Westminster Press, 1975).

[50]Clifford Green, Bonhoeffer: The Sociality of Christ and Humanity (Missoula, Montana: Scholars Press, 1972).

[51]Dissent, pp. 103, 104.

[52]Clifford Green, "Bonhoeffer in the Context of Erikson's Luther Study" in Psychohistory and Religion, ed. by Roger Johnson (Philadelphia: Fortress Press, 1977), p. 186.

[53]Revelation and the Secular in the Theology of Dietrich Bonhoeffer, pp. 14, 15.

[54]Ibid., p. 80.

[55]Ibid., pp. 72, 73.

[56]Kelley's definition of what would constitute a "break" in one's thought sets conditions which seem virtually impossible to meet. He writes, "Both Bonhoeffer's and his correspondent's lives are without definite breaks, except those each had deliberately chosen among alternatives at hand (p. 122)". When we speak of a break, we mean that Bonhoeffer after 1939 unambiguously affirms and develops a positive account of earthly life which is not to be found in his work before 1939. Specifically, he praises the value of personal longings and encourages Christians to feel their secular desires to the fullest. Insofar as this does not appear before 1939, we take it to be a break, or shift in the progression of Bonhoeffer's thought.

[57]Dietrich Bonhoeffer, pp. 606, 607.

[58]Ibid., p. 618.

[59]This diary entry is reproduced in Dietrich Bonhoeffer, p. 618.

[60]Ibid., p. 619.

[61]Gesammelte Schriften, Vol. I (Munich: Kaiser, 1965), pp. 377ff. Cf. Mary Bosanquet, The Life and Death of Dietrich Bonhoeffer (New York: Harper and Row, 1968), p. 228.

[62]Gesammelte Schriften, vol. I (Munich: Kaiser, 1965), p. 50. Translated by Bethge in Dietrich Bonhoeffer, p. 647.

[63]Letter of August 25, 1942, reproduced by Bethge in Dietrich Bonhoeffer, pp. 693, 694.

[64]Gesammelte Schriften, Vol. II (Munich: Kaiser, 1965), pp. 419ff. Translated by Bethge in Dietrich Bonhoeffer, pp. 694, 695.

[65]This letter of November 27, 1942 is also reproduced by Bethge in <u>Dietrich Bonhoeffer</u>, p. 695.

CHAPTER III
BONHOEFFER ON EARTHLY DESIRES IN HIS ETHICS:
MOVING TOWARD A SOLUTION TO THE PROBLEM

# I

As the previous chapters suggested, Bonhoeffer's affirmation in the Letters and Papers from Prison of the value and importance of desires for the good things of the earth for their own sake represents a major development in his theology, contrasting with his work before 1939. Bonhoeffer often encouraged Christians to love the earth prior to 1939, but it was always to be a love mediated in and through Christ.[1] At no time before 1939 did he encourage or urge purely human, secular desires for life's good things.[2] In fact, desires for earthly realities are addressed only rarely in the early writings, and such yearnings are repeatedly dismissed as sinful impulses which proceed from, and perpetuate, the condition of human fallenness. Their chief effect, according to the pre-1939 writings, is to draw persons away from God, weaken their devotion to His Lordship, and lead them unknowingly into the grasp of Satan.[3]

After 1939, Bonhoeffer elaborated a different and positive perspective on earthly desires. As we saw in the Letters, desires for the good things of the earth for their own sake are encouraged, extolled and urged. Feeling desires fully is an achievement which is said to enhance one's humanness and foster multi-dimensional Christian living. The Christian's love of God (cantus firmus) is not threatened by earthly desires; rather, it assists considerably to develop them "as powerfully as possible" and with "complete independence". In fact, earthly desires can only become whole and full, or as Bonhoeffer puts it, have a "full and perfect sound", when the cantus firmus lends it s firm support.[4] But this account leave unclear the nature of the "good" to be found in earthly life with its "complete independence" from the love of God. It also does not specify the nature of the goodness of desire itself. For if God alone is good, what "good" can there be in fallen earthly realities or in secular desires not mediated through Christ? Why does Bonhoeffer now encourage and urge longings which he had earlier condemned, accepting them simply as irremovable elements of fallen life? These ambiguities draw our attention to the Ethics, Bonhoeffer's unfinished magnum opus, written between the winter of 1939/1940 and his imprisonment in April of 1943. Here Bonhoeffer begins to express a more sympathetic perspective on earthly life as lived in relative abstraction from Christ. This in turn illuminates the statement about earthly desires later found in the Letters.

In order to trace the movement of Bonhoeffer's though from 1939 to the provocative insights of the prison writings, selected portions of the Ethics will be examined in chronological sequence.[5]

We will examine Bonhoeffer's treatment of fallen, earthly life in order to determine if, and in what sense, he assigns value to earthly realities. For if he affirms "good" or "value" in the life without God, he clarifies how he can rightfully urge and encourage a Christian to desire the good things of the earth for their own sake. The coherence of his thinking on these matters will be discussed in the concluding chapter of the study. Our approach to the Ethics will assume that Bonhoeffer did not radically alter his way of thinking in the five years during which he wrote the Ethics and the Letters and Papers from Prison. Thus, whenever a correspondence of ideas appears between the two texts, or whenever a correlation can logically be implied, I take the parallel to be in Bonhoeffer's mind, whether or not he explicitly makes the connections. This survey will include considerations of the nature of fallen reality, the penultimate/ultimate, the natural, bodily life, and life itself. Such an approach will connect the Ethics with the prison texts and elucidate the course of Bonhoeffer's thought up until his death. It should also suggest the direction which Bonhoeffer's work on desires might have taken had he been able to continue it.

At the outset of the Ethics, in a chapter entitled "The Love of God and the Decay of the World", Bonhoeffer discusses the Fall and the resultant nature of human, earthly life. Written during the year 1939/1940, this section echoes the pessimistic description of the Fall presented in The Cost of Discipleship and Creation and Fall. As in these earlier works, Bonhoeffer emphasizes here human fallenness and separation from God. He depicts in some detail human life amidst godless distinctions of good and evil which were introduced into existence through the rejection of God.[6] This chapter portrays fallen man as radically divorced from his Creator, as "apart from God, outside God".[7] In effect, man's grasping of the knowledge of good and evil has reversed his original knowledge of good and evil has reversed his original knowledge and severed him from the reconciling life in God. Where he had once known only God, man now knows only himself as his own creator and judge, and his own good and evil. But the good and evil he knows are not the good and evil of God; rather, they are in opposition to God, "against God".[8]

This chapter is almost entirely negative with respect to the subject of our inquiry. Bonhoeffer says nothing explicitly positive about human "good" or earthly values and, on occasion, he appears to deny it. But there are faint signs in the midst of this harsh appraisal of fallen man and his disordered life that perhaps a certain good and even a certain capacity to love persist in man nonetheless. Bonhoeffer does not affirm any earthly goodness explicitly, but he does not deny it when it would logically have followed to do so. The fact that these matters are only hinted at in Chapter I will be in marked contrast to the striking affirmations of human, earthly life and values which appear in subsequent chapters and in the Letters, and will lend support to our argument that Bonhoeffer's thought underwent a dramatic transformation in his last years.

For example, Bonhoeffer's account of shame contrasts sharply with his later affirmation of earthly longings. Shame, as he explains it, is man's recollection of his fallenness and his yearning to restore his lost unity (Gemeinschaft) with God and man. Shame longs for the fellowship with God and others which was man's to enjoy before the Fall. Yet when this yearning draws closest to its fulfillment, in both religious and human form, shame becomes most intense and "creates for itself the very deepest secrecy".[9] Man's effort to regain the unity lost in the Fall is thus futile without the assistance of God. This failure of human yearning to achieve its desires for absent loved ones do serve to restore human fellowship (Gemeinschaft) and help keep the bond between persons intact. Desiring others for their own sake successfully cements and even deepens human fellowship.[10] In the first chapter of the Ethics, shame may be said to have a creditable intention: "...it is grief for this estrangement, and the powerless longing to return to unity with the origin".[11] But Bonhoeffer presents only a negative appraisal of the human desires for others which give rise to shame.

Bonhoeffer's account of the chaotic life of the man of disunion is also strongly negative in its treatment of earthly good and value:

> ...for the man who is in disunion with God,
> all things are in disunion, what is and what
> should be, life and law, knowledge and action,
> idea and reality, reason and instinct, duty and
> inclination, conviction and advantage, necess-
> ity and freedom, exertion and genius, universal
> and concrete, individual and collective, even truth,
> justice, beauty and love come into opposition with
> one another, just as do pleasure and displeasure,
> happiness and sorrow. One could prolong the
> list still further...[12]

Fallen from his origin, the "pharisee's" life is thoroughly disordered. He now knows good and evil and "subordinates his entire life" to scrupulously seeking out the good, hoping thereby to satisfy the rigorous demand so his conscience and regain his lost unity.[13]

But the Pharisee fails to realize, because of the blindness of his unbelief, that his judgment "is itself apostasy",[14] and that his entire existence proceeds from, and confirms, his defection from his origin.[15]  Knowing of his own goodness, the Pharisee cannot know the will of God, for his knowledge is merely self-knowledge and therefore false.  Further, the good and evil he knows is also false, for it too arises from his disunion:

> Man knows good and evil, but because he is
> not the origin, because he acquires this knowl-
> edge only at the price of estrangement from
> the origin, the good and evil that he knows
> are not the good and evil of God but good and
> evil against God.  They are good and evil of man's
> choosing, in opposition to the eternal election
> of God.[16]

As a result of the Fall, the Pharisee knows only his own good and evil, and his attempts to restore his lost unity in the painstaking process of discerning and doing the good serve only to deepen the gulf between himself and God:

> ...indeed, the action which is intended to over-
> come the disunion of man in good and evil does
> not achieve this aim but only aggravates the dis-
> union still further.  And in this way, for the
> Pharisee, the doing of the good which is intended
> to heal the inner disunion of man and his dis-
> union with other men leads only to still greater
> disunion and to persistence in the defection from
> the origin.[17]

Knowing of his own goodness, therefore, the Pharisee is blind to the will of God, and has no knowledge of Jesus Christ.  Conversely, the believer who knows of Christ knows nothing of this human goodness, for Jesus "voids" it.[18]  This is crucial to our inquiry for, as we have seen, Bonhoeffer later argues that the believer can and should know the relative good of earthly life and is to commit himself to the life without God along with non-Christians.  Bonhoeffer has not implied such a relative goodness in fallen human actions in Chapter I, nor has he implied the possibility of such a life for the Christian.  At best, we say that he has not explicitly denied or excluded it.

74

The Pharisee's actions are uniformly described as conflicting with the will of God:

> The situation is quite clear: knowing of Jesus
> a man can no longer know of his own goodness,
> and knowing of his own goodness he can no
> longer know of Jesus. Man cannot live simul-
> taneously in reconciliation and disunion, in
> freedom and under the law, in simplicity and
> in discordancy. There are no intermediate
> stages here; it is one thing or the other.[19]

All of the Pharisee's actions are described as "false doing", "self-deception", and "hypocrisy", for they fundamentally proceed from the fallen will of man.[20] Even deeds performed with the finest of human motives are likewise condemned. Jesus will thoroughly reject all such actions, for they conflict with God's will, regardless of their professed allegiance to Christ:

> ...this profession may well spring from a per-
> sonally upright heart, and with this brave
> profession there may well be associated an equally
> brave an devoted action. This profession and
> ths action may arise from the determination of
> a steadfast character to give his support to that
> which he has recognized to be good. And yet Jesus
> will reject this profession and this action precisely
> because they arise from man's own knowledge
> of good and evil; for indeed what takes place here,
> even though it may bear a striking resemblance to
> the will of God, is fundamentally the will of man,
> who is in a state of disunion with God.[21]

Due to the Fall, these actions are devoid of goodness. Later, in Chapter IV, in his account of the Natural, Bonhoeffer will explain how actions can be absolutely without goodness and yet relatively good. But for now he sheds no light on the nature of fallen "good" or of its positive relationship to the good of God.

We see a similar rejection of earthly good in Bonhoeffer's treatment of love. Only God is love, and His love transcends all disunion and exceeds all that fallen man may mistake for it:

> ...it is of the essence of love that it should lie
> beyond all disunion. A love which violates or

even neutralizes truth is called by Luther,
with his clear biblical vision, an "accursed
love", even though it may present itself in the
most pious dress. A love which embraces only
the sphere of personal human relations and
which capitulates before the objective and the
real can never be the love of the New Testament.[22]

There is no implication here that God's love supports the love of "personal human relations", which is exactly what the <u>cantus firmus</u> will later do to the counterpoint of "earthly affection". Love is the reconciliation of man in Jesus Christ, and apart from God's revelation man cannot possess this love, produce it, or understand it. Its origin is not in the natural order, and man can only know love when he first knows God: "Only he who knows God knows what love is... Only in Jesus Christ do we know what love is, namely, in His deed for us".[23]

There are actions, convictions, affections and attitudes which are commonly called love, but they have nothing to do with the love of God. Bonhoeffer insists that "...there is no love which is free or independent from the love of God".[24] Love of God and neighbor is the Christian's love. He knows no other. That which others describe as love is fallen in character. Thus, there are two senses of the word love as there were two senses of good.[25] There is God's love, as defined in Christ and practiced by the faithful, and there is a fallen imitation of love practiced by those living in disunion.

This account of the two senses of the word "love" is in noticeable contrast to the sentiments expressed in Bonhoeffer's wedding sermon to Eberhard and Renate Bethge in May of 1943. There, as we saw, he spoke of their love as their own, affirmed by God, yet relatively independent from Him. At that time he argued that viewing the relationship differently would represent a grave misunderstanding:

It is obvious, and it should not be ignored,
that it is your own very human wills that are
at work here, celebrating their truimph; the
course that you are taking at the outset is one
that you have chosen for yourselves; what
you have done and are doing is not, in the first
place, something religious, but something
quite secular.. Unless you can boldly say today:
"That is <u>our</u> resolve, <u>our</u> love, <u>our</u> way", you

are taking refuge in a false piety. "Iron and steel may pass away, but our love shall abide for ever".[26]

But how are we to understand this love of which Bonhoeffer writes in 1943? In Chapter I of the Ethics, no such Christian love is discussed for all love is God's love and not an independent activity of the believer:

> ...everything which is to be said of human
> love... is governed by the principle that God is
> love. The love with which man loves God and
> his neighbor is the love of God and no other;
> for there is no other love; there is no love which
> is free or independent from the love of God.
> In this, then, the love of man remains purely
> passive. Loving God is simply the other aspect
> of being loved by God.[27]

Bonhoeffer does not recognize here a "relative independence" to earthly love. In fact, although it is not strictly forbidden, he encourages no love beside the love of Christ. How, then, are we to understand the love of which Bonhoeffer speaks in the sermon of 1943? It cannot be the Christian love, for no love, so understood, can be had apart from Christ. If it is a human "love", then what precisely is the "triumph" in that love which God affirms? In the Letters, Bonhoeffer writes:

> As God today adds his 'Yes' to your 'Yes', as
> he confirms your will with his will and as he
> allows you, and approves of, your triumph and
> rejoicing and pride, he makes you at the same
> time instruments of his will and purpose both
> for yourselves and for others.[28]

But why would God confirm the human will "with his will"? On what basis would God endorse a love which is not His own? Moreover, how can the Christian participate in the life without God, and "love" in relative freedom from God, without thereby falling more deeply into sin? These are questions which we will take up later. For now it is significant that Bonhoeffer in 1940 neither explicitly or implicitly endorses what he urged on Christians in 1943, namely, a human "love" relatively independent of Christ.

On the whole, Bonhoeffer simply re-states the traditional

Lutheran view of the Fall. Man is fallen, judged, and condemned apart from Christ, incapable of love until restored to God through faith. Only then can the believer partake of the love of God and convey that love to his neighbor. The man of faith alone is able to love, for the believer is a vessel through which the spirit of God's love can flow. There is no human love or human good worth taking seriously in its own right, but only fallen impostors which lead persons away from the reunion with God and others they seek. Thus, this human love and human good, because of their inferiority to their distinctively Christian counterparts, are not encouraged for their own sake.

But despite this dark account of the Pharisee, of earthly desires, and of human capabilities for "good" and "love", Bonhoeffer faintly implies that relative value can be found in human life apart from Christ. In his discussion of the higher motives which underlie human action, he speaks of fallen man possessing an "upright heart", engaging in "brave and devoted action", and also capable of deeds recognized in some sense as "good". He also recognizes that humans are able to "love" in some sense apart from Christ and His love. The chapter concludes in a similar vein: "Being loved by God does not by any means deprive man of his mighty thoughts and spirited deeds".[29] This suggests that even under God man's actions may possess a relative independence of value.

These remarks raise important questions. If the actions of the Pharisee are such that they can be known as good, as brave and devoted, and even as flowing from an upright heart, then there would seem to be some sense in which these actions are truly good or of value, although Bonhoeffer has labeled all such actions as false. Bonhoeffer may be obliquely referring to, or at least leaving open the possibility of, a relative goodness and love of which fallen man is capable, despite his actions being false in an absolute sense. But if Bonhoeffer is implying these relative values here at all, it is only in the weakest and most indirect fashion. He does not discuss this goodness any further, and no additional clarification of human goodness or of the mighty thoughts and spirited deeds of which fallen men are capable is provided in this chapter.

II

In his second chapter, "The Church and the World", which was completed by August of 1940, Bonhoeffer examines these "mighty thoughts" and "spirited deeds" of men in greater detail. Here he affirms earthly values more directly, unambiguously, and centrally than he did in Chapter I. Now he argues explicitly that some human values do, indeed, possess a relative worth in themselves, although still opposed to Christ and faith. In fact, despite their fallen nature, they are said to have "come very near indeed to the Christian standpoint", and are drawn to Christ:

> Reason, culture, humanity, tolerance and self-determination, all these concepts which until very recently had served as battle slogans against the Church, against Christianity, against Jesus Christ Himself, had now, suddenly and surprisingly, come very near indeed to the Christian standpoint...

> It is not Christ who must justify Himself before the world by the acknowledgment of the values of justice, truth and freedom, but it is these values which have come to need justification, and their justification can only be Jesus Christ.[30]

It is significant that Bonhoeffer refers to these humn concepts as "values" (Güter), despite their need for ultimate justification in Christ. Based upon his firm rejection of the Pharisee and his way of life, one might have expected Bonhoeffer to argue that Christ would deny the worth of these "values" and reject their pleas for justification. After all, they represent standards of human excellence, man's noblest and loftiest criteria for measuring the value of lives and cultures. They are the values toward which man strives when seeking to be at his best without the assistance of God. But, pursued apart from Christ, they remain man's standards of judgment and not God's. As such, they are in opposition to God and would presumably be worthy of condemnation. But despite their fallen character, they are values nevertheless, and Christ supports, protects, accepts responsibility for, and claims these values and those who strive to uphold them. He becomes a part of the human struggle on behalf of these earthly "values":

> Jesus gives His support to those who suffer for the sake of a just cause, even if this cause is not precisely the confession of His name; He takes them under His protection. He accepts responsibility for them, and He lays claim to them. And so the man who is persecuted for a just cause is led to Christ.[31]

Here, for the first time, we get an intimation of the thesis that Christian faith urges and encourages believers to take human values seriously. For if human values are given support by Christ, it would follow that the believer, in seeking to be Christ-like, would similarly lend his aid to earthly causes and values.

In effect, Bonhoeffer provides a vindication of sorts for the Pharisee. The actions of the "man of disunion" remain the product of his fallenness and face ultimate condemnation as "false action" and "hypocrisy", but they are also granted a value in some sense, and those who perform such actions are supported by Christ. There is a certain value attached to being "righteous" in the world, although doing so apart from Christ.

> ...out time must say... that before a man can
> know and find Christ he must first become
> righteous like those who strive and who suffer
> for the sake of justice, truth and humanity...
> Christ belongs to both the wicked and the good;
> He belongs to them both only as sinners, that is
> to say, as men who in their wickedness and in
> their goodness have fallen away from the origin.
> He summons them back to the origin so that they
> shall no longer be good and evil but justified and
> sanctified sinners. But before we express this ul-
> timate in which evil and good are one before Christ
> and in which the difference between all times
> is annulled before Christ, we must not avoid
> the question which is set us by out experience and
> by out time, the question of what is meant by saying
> that the good find Christ, in other words the re-
> lationship of Jesus Christ to good people and to
> goodness.[32]

The dialectic of earthly life thus makes it possible for actions to possess a certain "goodness" or "wickedness" while, at the same time, being broadly categorized as sinful and wicked in nature.[33] While persons shall no longer be good and evil once they are Christians, Bonhoeffer will argue that they must know and perform the relative good of earthly life.

Bonhoeffer here acknowledges the existence of "good" people outside of the Church, and writes explicitly for the first time of a "goodness" relatively independent of Christ.

> Good, in this sense, contains an extremely
> wide range of gradations, extending from the
> purely external observance of good order to the

most intimate self-examination and character-
formation and to personal self-sacrifice for the
most sublime human values.[34]

He refers here to those who have fallen away from their origin but
whose way of life sets them on an ethical plane far surpassing those
who live in wickedness.[35]

Bonhoeffer clearly believed that he was introducing something new to Reformation theology. He insists that the "good" of
which he speaks is not produced by the Holy Spirit, nor is it merely a
form of noble sinfulness carried out by the heathen.[36] It is a genuine
"good", which is somehow independent of the righteousness of
God.[37] It is a "good" which must be recognized by Chrisitan faith if
the relationship of Jesus Christ to such "good" people is to be repre-
sented accurately.

Over and over again the Church, when she has
based herself upon Scripture, has given thought
to the relationship of Jesus Christ to the wicked
and to wickedness. In the Churches of the Reformation this question has been predominant;
and indeed one of the decisive achievements of
the Reformation was that in this connection it
spoke the word of the gospel with all the depth
and fullness of the New Testament. Yet the
question of the relationship of the good man to
Christ remained remarkably neglected.[38]

Bonhoeffer's point, not previously elaborated and appreciated in
Reformation theology, is that such "goodness" demands attention
and respect just as it is claimed by Christ. Christian ridicule and
unrelenting condemnation of "good" people and their actions reveals
a misunderstanding of the claim of Christ, the dialectic of human
life and of the meaning of good citizenship.

Bonhoeffer explains why a shift in the traditional account of
human "good" is required when he writes of the total and exclusive
claims of Christ. Once again, the dialectic inherent in earthly life is
emphasized. On the one hand, he argues that Jesus "defines the
limits of membership in Himself more widely than His disciples
wish Him to do or themselves do".[39] As we have seen, Christ is
willing to claim as His those who sacrifice themselves for justice,
truth, humanity and freedom; in fact, he takes responsibility for
them and the values for which they stand. But, at the same time,

Jesus strictly warns that "He that is not with me is against me (Matt. 12:30)".  Bonhoeffer admits that these two emphases appear to be in "irreconcilable contradiction", but that "living experience" has proven that they belong together.[40]  He explains that the Church appropriately responded to the threats of anti-Christian forces by requiring a total devotion to the Church and its Lord.  Neutrality and weakness of faith had permitted the erosion of the community of faith, and led to the call for a clear and undivided profession of allegiance to Christ.[41]  Yet it was precisely when the Church took seriously the severity of Christ's claim to exclusivity that it discovered the freedom and the confidence to open itself to the world:

> ...precisely through this concentration on the
> essential, the Church acquired and inward
> freedom and breadth which preserved her against
> any timid impulse to draw narrow limits, and
> there gathered around her men who came from
> very far away, and men to whom she could
> not refuse her fellowship and her protection;
> injured justice, oppressed truth, vilified hu-
> manity and violated freedom all sought for
> her, or rather for her Master, Jesus Christ.[42]

Having experienced first the necessity of exclusiveness, the Church now "had the living experience of that other saying of Jesus: 'He that is not against us is for us'".[43]

The two claims of Christ must remain in a dialectic relation-ship.  Each requires the corrective of the other.  In isolation, the claim to exclusiveness leads to "fanaticism and slavery", and the claim to totality slips into the "secularization and self-abandonment of the Church".[44]  Bonhoeffer now argues, in contrast to earlier statements, that the claim to exclusiveness, rightly understood, does not draw Christ and His people out of the world, but reveals more clearly than ever the breadth of His dominion in the world.[45]  When understood in their unity, the two claims prevent unqualified con-demnation of all actions conducted apart from Christ, and require instead that their relative worth be granted.

In Chapter II, Bonhoeffer writes primarily about the unbe-liever, but the significance of the chapter for Christians is unmis-takable.  The human "good" of which Bonhoeffer writes is discernible apart from God, for the unbeliever discerns it.  Yet it is affirmed by Christ, Who supports, claims, protects and takes responsibility for both earthly values and the persons who strive to uphold them.  By extension, we would expect that the Christian should likewise lend his assistance to the fostering of earthly values, although Bonhoeffer has not stated it explicitly. With these affirmations, Bonhoeffer is moving beyond the negative focus of the previous chapter, and taking the first steps toward his later encouraging and urging of Christians to desire the good things of the earth for their own sake.

III

The theme of earthly good is pursued in Chapter III, "Ethics as Formation", [46] wherein describes human life as enveloped in the tension of Christ's incarnation and crucifixion. In a tone reminiscent of his Christology lectures of 1933,[47] and further removed from the one-sided emphasis of The Cost of Discipleship and Life Together, Bonhoeffer stresses the reconciliation of God and the world as wrought in Christ. But in contrast to the Christology lectures, wherein Christ's mediating presence took form in human society, history and nature, the reconciled world in Chapter III of the Ethics retains a certain godless independence over against His reconciliation. The world is accepted and reconciled, but continues to oppose Christ and His purposes nevertheless. The redeeming Christ unifies reality and takes His place at the center of nature, history and man, but the fallen world continues to resist Him with relative integrity:

> God loves man. God loves the world. It is not
> an ideal man that he loves, but man as he is;
> not an ideal world, but the real world. What
> we find abominable in man's opposition to
> God, what we shrink back from with pain and
> hostility, the real man, the real world, this is
> for God the ground for unfathomable love, and
> it is with this that He unites Himself utterly.
> God becomes man, real man. While we are
> trying to grow out beyond our manhood, to
> leave the man behind us, God becomes man and
> we have to recognize that God wishes us men,
> too, to be real men.[48]

Christ's reconciliatory presence in the midst of reality, reality loved despite its persistent fallenness, places earthly life in the grip of an on-going tension which defines life itself:

> The "yes" and the "no" which God addresses to
> history in the incarnation and crucifixion of
> Jesus Christ introduces into every historical

instant an infinite and unresolvable tension.
History does not become a transient vehicle,
but through the life and death of Jesus Christ
it does for the first time become truly temporal.
It is precisely in its temporality that it is history
with God's consent.[49]

The cross serves as reminder of God's judgment upon human reality and its failings; yet the incarnation and resurrection simultaneously speak of God's affirmation of earthly values. There is no intrinsic value in fallen life, for it has despised its origin and cast God out of its presence. Before the crucified God, fallen life is utterly godless and sinful.[50]

Yet, in the incarnation and resurrection, God gives life back through the same person of Christ. He speaks a "yes" to sinful life now reconciled and a "yes" to the good things preserved within that life, though it is still in itself sinful and godless. The "no" and the "yes" must be heard together. A diminution or elimination of either the "yes" or the "no" upsets the balance upon which earthly life depends and out of which the "real man" lives.[51] One must not clutch at life convulsively, ignoring God's "no", nor cast it aside, deaf to His "yes".[52] Instead, one takes what life offers by taking seriously God's judgment and the incarnation and resurrection in which Christ affirms life and gives it back to man:

> ...whenever it is recognized that the power of
> death has been broken, wherever the world of
> death is illumined by the miracle of the resur-
> rection and of the new life, there no eternities
> are demanded of life but one takes of life what
> it offers, not all or nothing, but good and evil,
> the important and the unimportant, joy and
> sorrow; one neither clings convulsively to life
> not its allotted span and one does not invest
> earthly things with the title of eternity...[53]

Here Bonhoeffer once more affirms the presence of "good" in earthly life, of things which are important and joy-producing. But he has added something as yet unknown to his corpus. For the first time, he begins to encourage the Christian to accept earthly life in its wholeness. What he had implied in Chapter II, he now states explicitly: the believer is to follow the example of Christ in accepting earthly life even in its fallenness. Since Christ has accepted and reconciled all of earthly life, the Christian is to do likewise, taking what that life has to offer, including its godlessness and wickedness.

While accepting fallen life in its godlessness, Christ's presence grips and defines earthly reality in the tension of both His judgment and His redemption. God loves precisely that which opposes Him, and Christians are to do the same, with a human love. Those who would accuse and shrink back from the godless world are confronted with Christ, the "real man", who became a "companion of sinners"[54] and beckons believers to follow. Christians are to love the world in its totality, in its "good and evil, the important and the unimportant, joy and sorrow".[55] This is a major step forward in Bonhoeffer's thinking, and the first encouragement for the Christian to enjoy earthly reality in its fallenness.

It is essential to point out, however, that Bonhoeffer has not yet defined the nature of the "good" which persists in earthly life, nor has he begun to explain how faith aids the Christian to experience these "goods" while living out of his knowledge of the goodness of God. But Bonhoeffer has explained that Christ now accepts the world in its fallenness and places life in the tension of His "yes" and "no" to earthly reality. Life in its wholeness is accepted by Christ, and is to be accepted by the believer as well. This is the beginning of Bonhoeffer's encouragement to the Christian to enjoy the good things of the earth for their own sakes, and it sheds some light upon the basis for Bethge's secular longing for Renate and of the other longings for the good things of the earth which Bonhoeffer urges in the Letters. In Chapter IV of the Ethics, we will see Bonhoeffer dramatically build upon Chapter III and offer more explicit support for earthly life and personal longings.

IV

In Chapter IV, "The Last Things and the Things Before the Last", Bonhoeffer presses ahead with his inquiry into the "unresolvable tension" which grips life through the incarnation and crucifixion of Jesus Christ.[56] His purpose is to clarify the nature of human life as it moves ahead in history under the "yes" and "no" addressed to it by God. In his discussion of the ultimate/penultimate, the natural, the rights of natural life and bodily joys, Bonhoeffer unambiguously begins to structure an account of earthly life which will ground his affirmation of fallen reality and the Christian's participation in that reality for its own sake.

Human life, understood by itself, is a "dark pit... inwardly and outwardly barred, sinking ever more hopelessly and inescapably in the abyss".[57] Without the life, death and resurrection of Jesus Christ, a life is "unjustified before God" and "delivered up to death and damnation".[58] But a Christian knows that his life has been "torn open by main force", as the "Word of God breaks in".[59] A person's encounter with Jesus Christ reveals to him that his life has previously been founded upon allegiance to himself or to a false god of his own imagining.[60] The word of God calls for a "complete breaking off of everything that precedes it", and a re-founding of one's life upon the person of Jesus Christ.[61] This "last word", which proceeds only from the free act of God, is defined as the "ultimate", and passes judgment upon the "penultimate", or "everything that precedes the justification of the sinner by grace alone, everything which is to be regarded as leading up to the last thing when the last thing has been found".[62] Justification is, "in every respect" that last word spoken to man,[63] and because this is so the things before the last cannot be said to have "any value of their own".[64] The penultimate remains, but the ultimate "entirely annuls and invalidates it". Henceforward, its value is to be understood in the light of its relationship to the ultimate.

But this account does not represent a call to pietistic excapism, or to an other-wordly asceticism. The ultimate and penultimate abide together as the constitutive elements in a world reconciled and united in Christ. This presents a dilemma to Christian living.[65] Namely, how is one to integrate one's commitment to the ultimate and the eternal with one's life in time, amid the penultimate? Bonhoeffer poses the question of the Christian's allegiance to the penultimate in this way: "We are asking, therefore, about the penultimate in the lives of Christians. We are asking whether to deny it is pious self-deception, or whether to take it seriously in its own way is to incur guilt".[66]

Previously, Bonhoeffer had argued that the things of earth, now categorized under the penultimate, were to be sought and enjoyed only with reference to Christ. Direct, immmediate relationships with earthly goods were forbidden, or, if unavoidably necessary, tolerated, for such relationships manifested a refusal to accept the mediating presence of Christ between man and the world. Now Bonhoeffer will encourage the believer to take the penultimate seriously "in its own way", in relative abstraction from the mediation and purposes of Christ. Bonhoeffer goes on to answer affirmatively the question whether the penultimate should be taken seriously in its own way. Bonhoeffer has thus left behind his notion that the believer must separate himself from the world, or love it solely on account of Christ. Now, through the mediation of Christ, he is prepared to consider the Christian's participation in life and its good things for their own sake, a proposal offered nowhere else in his writings before 1939. His account of the Christian life will no longer fix on the "breach" between Christ and the world,[67] but will be more thorough, nuanced, and positive with respect to earthly life.

In answer to his own question, Bonhoeffer discusses, and rejects, what he calls two "extreme solutions" to the problem.[68] One seeks to resolve the dilemma "radically"; the other by means of "compromise". The first, or radical solution, calls for the complete breaking off of contact with the penultimate.[69] It views all of life as either for or against Christ and regards the penultimate as a realm set against the word of grace and already judged. As a result, the "radical" acknowledges no Christian responsibility towards the world and its order, for all "is enmity towards Christ" and "ripe for burning".[70]

The "compromise" solution separates the ultimate word from all that goes before it, and grants the penultimate a right on its own account. The penultimate is "not threatened or imperilled by the ultimate".[71] This removal of the ultimate from the daily world of the penultimate serves, in effect, as "an eternal justification for things as they are".[72] "Compromise" effectively stills the voice of judgment which the ultimate attempts to speak to the world.

Both solutions, however, mistakenly regard the ultimate and penultimate as mutually exclusive categories, and fail to acknowledge their essential unity in God's creative and redemptive activities. The "radical" solution knows God only as Judge and Redeemer. His creation is viewed as a realm of evil, antithetical to his purposes. As such, it poses a constant threat to the Christian and becomes the object of his hatred. "Compromise", on the other hand, refuses to hear the call to renunciation and detachment from the world as sounded by the ultimate. "Compromise" hates the ultimate, denouncing it as "unnatural estrangement from the world and from men, and even as hostility towards them".[73] It promotes adaptability, worldly-wise prudence and discretion as Christian virtues.

Both solutions, therefore, must be discarded. As we will see in Chapter VI of the Ethics, these solutions fail because they do not heed both the "yes" and the "no" which God addresses to fallen life. Rightly understood, life is characterized by both the absolute distinction of the penultimate and the ultimate and by their unceasing interpenetration. An accurate rendering of life must be dialectical. Life in the world is too rich and nuanced in Christ to be described in so one-dimensional a manner: "There is no Christianity in itself, for this would destroy the world; there is no man in himself, he would exclude God. Both of these are merely ideas..."[74] The only true picture of reality is that found in Christ. In His incarnation, the love of God for the creation is expressed; His crucifixion reveals the judgment of God upon all flesh, and His resurrection proclaims the redemptive purpose of God for the world.[75] These elements cannot be separated. Together they speak of the will of God for created reality. To stress one aspect of His will at the expense of others is to distort the created and preserved reality entered by God. The cross pronounces the verdict of death upon the world as fallen from its origin, but the resurrection puts an end to death and calls forth new life.[76] Any view of the relationship of the ultimate and the penultimate which denies this abiding tension misrepresents the presence of God in the world:

> He [Jesus] neither renders the human reality
> independent nor destroys it, but He allows it
> to remain as that which is before the last, as
> a penultimate which requires to be taken ser-
> iously in its own way, and yet not to be taken
> seriously, a penultimate which has become
> the outer covering of the ultimate.[77]

Bonhoeffer now begins to answer his own question about taking the penultimate "seriously in its own way" in the affirmative. He implies that the good which persists in fallen life, while not fully independent of Christ, possesses a relative integrity and is to be respected by the believer. This suggests a certain seriousness or value in the penultimate, which is a departure from the substance and tone of his work before 1939. The appropriate answer, then, to the question as earlier posed is that the Christian, though cognizant of, and committed to the ultimate, can never either single-mindedly ignore or endorse the penultimate.[78] Instead, the believer should take the penultimate seriously, fully aware of its status as an "empty jest" in relation to the ultimate,[79] and yet committed to it on its own terms nevertheless. In effect, we see Bonhoeffer urging the Christian to respect fallen, earthly life, recognizing the relative value of the penultimate while, at the same time, acknowledging that it is of no value in the light of the ultimate.

The Christian is also duty-bound to preserve the penultimate for the sake of the ultimate. Herein lies a task for believers who desire the unhindered proclamation of the word of grace. It is essential that the penultimate be nourished in order that the ultim-

ate can be heard. Specifically, the content of the penultimate is epitomized as follows: "Concretely, two things are called penultimate in
relation to the justification of the sinner by grace, namely being
human (Menschsein) and being good".[80] As examples, Bonhoeffer
states that the way is prepared for the coming of Christ when the
hungry are fed, the homeless provided shelters, the lonely offered
fellowship, and the like. Persons must never be treated as means,
nor the established orders arbitrarily violated, for this impedes the
reception of Christ.[81] It makes a difference, even in the midst of "the
fallen, lost world",[82] that distinctions between good and evil be recognized and that the penultimate be attended to seriously.[83] Although it remains "an empty jest" in comparison with the ultimate,
the penultimate must be "respected and validated".[84] It retains a
relative right, and possesses and earnestness and validity of its
own.[85] In his account of the penultimate, Bonhoeffer affirms the relative good which remains in earthly life, the seriousness with which
the believer should treat this goodness, and the relative "earnestness
and validity" which the penultimate enjoys in relative abstraction
from Jesus Christ and His purposes. Here, and throughout Chapter
IV, we see Bonhoeffer providing a theological foundation for Christian participation in earthly life in its wholeness, which he had begun to encourage implicitly in Chapter III.

For the first time, Bonhoeffer insists that the Christian live
the earthly pole of the dialectic established by the person and work of
Christ. In earlier writings, notably his work from Barcelona in 1929,
Bonhoeffer wrote of this dialectic but did not encourage the believer's
participation in the fallen, earthly pole.[86] Now he does so explicitly
and unambiguously.

Life in itself is fallen, but at the same time it is preserved for,
and reconciled in, Jesus Christ. In an absolute sense, nothing in life
can be said to be of worth, for life is fallen from its origin, and only
Good is good. Yet there are distinctions between "good" and "evil" in
the penultimate. Therefore, Bonhoeffer is able to affirm human
goodness and argue that it is to be taken seriously by the Christian
and respected in itself. This departs from his work before 1939 and
from his earlier work in the Ethics.[87]

> Whatever humanity and goodness is found in
> this fallen world must be on the side of Jesus
> Christ... Certainly the humanity and goodness
> of which we are speaking are not the humanity
> and goodness of Jesus Christ; they cannot stand
> before the judgment; and yet Christ loved the

young man who had kept the commandments
(Mark 10:17ff.). Humanity and goodness should
not acquire a value on their own account, but the
should and shall be claimed for Jesus Christ,
especially in cases where they persist as the un-
conscious residue of a former attachment to the
ultimate.[88]

His treatment of the rich young ruler indicates that Bonhoeffer wishes to affirm a "goodness" in secular reality apart from God.
It is a goodness which persists in the fallen world, and provides an
opportunity for persons such as the young ruler to foster the "humanity" and "goodness" in their lives. This goodness is not the goodness of Christ; it is not above reproach in itself. But it is a goodness
which possesses a relative worth apart from God. Jesus loves the
rich young ruler, at least in part, because he has helped promote life
in the penultimate.

This account of the young ruler is a departure from Bonhoeffer's earlier treatment of the Pharisee. Earlier in the Ethics, Bonhoeffer had spoken harshly of the man who clings to his knowledge
of good and evil, and had given no indication that the good known
was in any sense real good. But now he does affirm it. The Pharisee's attempt to satisfy the demands of his own conscience and restore his lost unity in the painstaking process of discerning and doing the "good" had served only to deepen the gulf between himself
and God.[89] Bonhoeffer made no explicit mention of a relative goodness related to the preservation of the penultimate which is commendable in itself though fallen, although he did not deny it. Human action was categorized more broadly as an either-or. All action,
he argued, which was without Christ as its source was false action;
all of the Pharisee's actions were therefore described as "false
doing", "self-deception", and "hypocrisy".[90] But while he was not
willing explicitly to ascribe any relative goodness to the Pharisee, he
now ascribes it to the young ruler.

In terms of their absolute relationship to God, the Pharisee
and the young ruler are likewise condemned. Both live out their
knowledge of good and evil, and for them both all things are drawn
into the morass of their essential disunion. Both are "admirable"[91]
in their capacity to make sensitive judgments regarding good and
evil[92] and in their devotion to the carrying out of "right" action.[93]
The rich young ruler, like the Pharisee, has failed to undergo "a
complete transmutation" of his person, a "renewing of mind".[94] He,
too, is without faith. Yet Bonhoeffer does not speak of the young

man's goodness as a manifestation of his apostasy, nor of his ultimate condemnation. Instead, Bonhoeffer states that the young ruler, like Germans of Bonhoeffer's time, came to Jesus because he was "good".

It is Bonhoeffer's willingness to speak explicitly and unambiguously of the relative goodness of his actions which distinguishes the young man from the Pharisee and indicates a significant movement in Bonhoeffer's thought. The "goodness" attributed to the young man presumably confirms him in his disunion, and separates him from God, yet has a right of its own, and should be taken seriously and respected. Bonhoeffer's explanation of these two senses of the word "good" is new to his corpus and crucial to our inquiry. Bonhoeffer does not characterize this relative "goodness" as an evil which God later turns to good. Nor is Christ's love for the young man described as His general love for sinful mankind. Each of these characterizations would have been more traditionally Lutheran and in keeping with his earlier thought. But the goodness which Bonhoeffer attributes to the young ruler is indeed a form of good, and not merely a lesser evil. It is "good" that Christ recognizes, yet it is a property of man. It is man's good, not the good of Christ, but good nevertheless. Bonhoeffer must now clarify the nature of this "goodness" and explain how fallen man can produce such "goodness" in the absence of God.

In his section on The Natural, which follows immediately, Bonhoeffer begins to address these matters, and to establish some connections with what we have already seen in the Letters and Papers from Prison. While the penultimate is said to possess no ultimate value, distinctions between "good" and "evil" must be made under the heading of the "natural". Bonhoeffer laments that the concept of the natural has fallen into "discredit" in Protestant ethics.[95]

The Protestant tradition, he argues, devalued the human and earthly in its preoccupation with the "darkness of general sinfulness".[96] As a result, the relative goodness of certain earthly realities was lost in the negative filter of the Reform. The desire to protect the sovereignty and integrity of grace from the undermining influence of a natural theology was well-intentioned, but it left Protestant ethics unable to direct believer sin matters of practical, natural life. Since the sole antithesis to the natural was the word of grace, both the natural and the unnatural were equally condemned, and Protestant ethics could not speak in support of the former:

> Before the light of grace everything human
> and natural sank into the night of sin, and now

no one dared to consider the relative differences
differences within the human and the natural,
for fear that by their so doing grace as grace
might be diminished.[97]

Bonhoeffer therefore feels that it is imperative to restore the
perspective of the natural to the discourse of Protestant ethics. By
using the term "natural", Bonhoeffer wishes to account for the seriousness of the Fall. The concept of the natural is distinguishable
form the concept of the creaturely because it includes an "element of
independence (Eigenständigkeit) and self-development" (Eigenent-
wicklung) and freedom which is entailed in man's assertion of
himself in the Fall.[98] Through the Fall, through man's decision to
establish himself as his own origin, the "creature" forfeited his
absolute freedom before God and became "nature". This radically
altered the relationship of the Creator to creature, now become
nature, and posited a new freedom in the fallen world. This freedom
permits man to lend his aid and support to the natural, or to
withdraw it. His commitment to "humanity" and "goodness" promotes the natural, while his doing of the "evil", or his refusal to respect the penultimate is detrimental to the natural. It is the proper
use of misuse of this freedom in fallen life which constitutes the
distinction between good and evil. This freedom is identical to the
independence (Selbständigkeit) enjoyed by the counterpoints in
relation to the cantus firmus.

The direct dependence of the creature upon God is replaced by
the relative freedom of natural life. Within this freedom, there are
differences between the true and mistaken use of freedom, and there
is therefore the difference between the natural and the unnatural.
Insofar as the protection and promotion of the natural makes
possible the coming of grace, human response to the natural creates
a relative openness and a relative closeness for Christ.[99]

This relative freedom from Christ, and for others, must not be
confused with the absolute freedom for God and one's neighbor as
possessed by the believer. Only the word of grace can "create and
bestow" such freedom. The difference between the natural and the
unnatural is only relative, in that the openness of the natural to the
coming of Christ cannot, in itself, produce the coming of Christ from
below, nor can the closedness of the unnatural prevent it. But the
arrival of Christ reveals the natural as penultimate to His coming,
and the unnatural as destructive of it: "...Thus, even in the sight of
Christ, there is a distinction between the natural and the unnatural,
a distinction which cannot be obliterated without doing grave

harm".[100]

The natural, then, is a kind of dynamic preservative, put in place by God Himself, Who desires and values life[101] and wishes it preserved.[102] It is the form of life preserved for the fallen world and directed towards "justification, redemption and renewal through Christ".[103] What this means is that the natural is determined according to both its form and its contents.[104] Formally, it owes its existence to the will of God, under Whose direction it moves life towards the coming of Christ. With respect to its contents, the natural is the "form of the preserved life itself, which embraces the entire human race".[105]

Fallen man, according to Bonhoeffer, has lost the ability to discern the source of the natural forms which undergird his existence. But his reason is preserved and peculiarly suited for recognizing the universal nature of the forms themselves. Even in the absence of any acknowledgment of the higher ends it serves, man's reason tells him of the value of the natural as supportive of and intrinsically forming life.[106] Man, therefore, does what is relatively "good" or "evil" insofar as he serves or hinders the natural. This further explains, then, the nature of the goodness which Bonhoeffer attributes to the rich young ruler, the goodness which Jesus loved. Even though he lacked faith, the young man devoted himself to the natural in preserved life. His goodness consisted in his commitment to the good things of this worldly life as put in place by God and as perceived by his reason. It is these same good things of the earth, recognized by all, which the Christian is later encouraged to seek for their own sakes, without direct reference to Christ.

But preserved life is not protected only by the assent of man's reason. The natural also receives the approval of what Bonhoeffer calls the "underlying will" of preserved life,[107] so that forces doing violence or injury to the natural will, in the long run, suffer for it.[108] This "underlying will" directs itself "exclusively towards the contents, the non-formal aspects of the natural".[109] This exclusive direction is a result of the Fall. But it recognizes the natural as that which protects life, and provides it with and inner force, a kind of "strength" which resists harmful elements and safeguards it from the unnatural.[110] The "underlying will" of preserved life affirms and tends into the natural because of its preservative function. So, generally speaking, "life is its own physician", capable of purging itself of destructive forces.[111] Innately forceful on its own behalf, life resists the unnatural and fosters the natural, thereby serving the purposes of God and enriching the quality of life as well.

Natural life, then, is "formed life".[112] It is life shaped by the natural, and served and protected by it. When life adheres to this given form, it is enhanced, but when the natural is abandoned, life is threatened with disintegration. Life in itself, abstracted from the innate support of the natural is "a void, a plunge into the abyss".[113] Though life in itself remains what Bonhoeffer had earlier called it, "a dark pit...sinking hopelessly and inescapably in the abyss", the natural endows it with a form and an inherent direction from which it cannot be abstracted. The natural constitutes a relative "good" in the life torn loose from its source. Individual attentiveness to that good is an end in itself and also advances the further purposes of God. We begin to see here, in part, why Bonhoeffer encourages devotion to the natural: it is in accord with the will and thrust of created life itself to do so. Life itself is served when persons seek the natural, and individuals and community life are better for it.

For this reason, Bonhoeffer rejects notions of life which misrepresent the natural. He rejects "vitalism" which absolutizes the correct insight that life is an end in itself. Vitalism divorces life from its form and purpose, posits life as an absolute, and ends in nihilism and destruction. Life's form places life in the service of others, and in this sense shapes life as a means to an end. When man fails to acknowledge this fact of formed life, he breaks life off from its system of support and "destroys" it "to the very roots".[114] At the other extreme is the threat of "mechanization" which absolutizes the correct insight that life is a means to an end. Individuals and communities are viewed only with respect to their utilizability for higher purposes. Life becomes enslaved to its form, and the freedom of formed life is extinguished. Bound in the error of mechanization, life no longer possesses its right as an end in itself.[115]

Natural life, in reality, avoids these two extremes. It serves as a means to an end in its duties to others and, though it does not know it, in preserving life for the ultimate. It also remains an end in itself in its rights for full, free life[116] and, though it does not know it, in enjoying its creaturehood. With reference to Christ, life as an end in itself is understood as creaturehood; persons are free to enjoy the earth's good things as created on their behalf. When viewed as a means to an end, it is understood as "participation in the kingdom of God...",[117] the conscious carrying out of His higher purposes. As an end in itself, life is endowed with certain rights, and, insofar as it serves as a means to and end, it is also placed under the obligation to fulfill certain duties. If either the rights or the duties are given undivided consideration, without respect or regard for the other, the bonding of rights and duties which holds preserved life together will be undone, and life will face the threat of collapse. Rights do enjoy a priority of sorts, however, inasmuch as it is from the rights given to life that the duties proceed.

The rights of natural life are the gifts of God which are "in the midst of the fallen world the reflected splendour of the glory of God's creation".[118] From this perspective, the rights are both ends in themselves and means to an end. They are ends in themselves in that they permit and encourage persons to relate to others and to enjoy life itself. But precisely because they are ends in themselves, they also serve as means tò the end of directing man's attention to their source. The duties, as Bonhoeffer's explains, "derive" from the rights, "as tasks are implied by gifts".[119]

> Within the framework of the natural life,
> therefore, we in every case speak first of the
> rights and then of the duties, for by so doing,
> in the natural life too, we are allowing the
> gospel to have its way.[120]

For our present purposes, then, it is the rights of natural life, and the freedom they enjoy, which are of primary significance, because they are new to Bonhoeffer's thought and crucial to the course of our inquiry.

Bonhoeffer's assertion that the rights of natural life are "gifts" of God is another advance in his unfolding argument. For the characterization of these rights as gifts strongly implies an intrinsic value or goodness in the gifts themselves, inasmuch as God would not logically be the giver of evil gifts and gifts would not be gifts unless they possessed intrinsic worth. Bonhoeffer suggests as much also when he states that these gifts reflect the "splendour of the glory of God's creation". Nowhere earlier in his writings does Bonhoeffer ascribe such intrinsic value to fallen, earthly life. In fact, it is noticeably absent in Creation and Fall where it would logically and theologically fit into his discussion.[121]

Fundamental to the free exercise of all natural rights is the preeminent right to bodily life. Bodily life, because it is the form chosen by God for human temporal and eternal life, possesses an "innate" right to be preserved.[122] Since the body is of particular significance as the form in which human life is perpetuated, it is not merely an adornment or subordinate to higher ends, but is an end in itself:

> Bodiliness and human life belong inseparably
> together. And thus the bodiliness which is
> willed by God to be the form of existence of
> man is entitled to be called an end in itself
> within the natural life. If the body were only
> a means to an end man would have no right to
> bodily joys.[123]

The body is still subordinate to the ultimate purposes for which it was designed by God. But the body also has a right to joys and pleasures which can be sought and appreciated without consideration of these higher ends. Bonhoeffer offers practical examples of this thesis. The right of the body to pleasure, for example, includes the right to play. Play ceases to be play when subordinated to more serious ends, for the nature of play lies in its purposelessness. In like fashion, the Christian is not required to eat and drink solely for the purpose of maintaining bodily health. There is a pleasure inherent in eating and drinking, a pleasure which is to be enjoyed for its own sake. Sex, also, is not meant only to serve the purpose of procreation. Husbands and wives can, and should, enjoy their sexuality simply for the pleasure it gives them. The same principle applies to one's life at home. Home is not merely a place which affords protection and an environment for the raising of children, but is a setting in which one can rightly savor the pleasures of "his personal life in the intimacy and security of his family and property".[124] Clothing, too, can be worn not only as a covering or as a protection against the elements, but as an adornment to be appreciated in itself. Various human bodily activities are indeed in the service of God's final purposes for man, but they also serve the limited end of bringing pleasure to the person for its own sake:

> From all this it emerges that the meaning of
> bodily life never lies solely in its subordination
> to its final purpose. The life of the body assumes
> its full significance only with the fulfillment
> of its inherent claim to joy.[125]

There is, then, a "goodness" disclosed by experience in the enjoyment of bodily pleasures for their own sake. These joys, Bonhoeffer argues, may seem "jejune and unheroic" to some, but are God's gifts to man and an integral part of life. They are meant to be sought and appreciated as ends in themselves.[126] Implied in the gifts of the body and their attendant rights is the encouragement to enjoy the gifts as a "good", for their own sake.

96

Several questions arise from this preliminary discussion of rights. As Bonhoeffer explains it, God gives as His gifts the rights with which natural life is endowed.[127] Through faith, the Christian also knows these joys to be "the reflected splendour of the glory of God's creation". But Bonhoeffer says something more. Even the unbeliever, lacking the vision of faith, is capable of recognizing the rights inherent in life, though he cannot know them as gifts. Unable to acknowledge to rights as come from God, the unbeliever is nevertheless expected to perceive and respect the rights given to life:

> Within natural life, therefore, it is incumbent
> upon reason to take account of the right of the
> individual, even though the divine origin of
> this right is not recognized.[128]

But how can reason accomplish this task, if the only basis for the rights is hidden from its view? How can reason acknowledge the rights of the natural if it cannot know their theological foundation? If reason is to recognize and respect individual rights, then there must be evidence to which reason has access which establishes these rights. Bonhoeffer explains that reason is by nature particularly suited for discerning the universal in what it perceives. Apparently following a Kantian model, he claims that reason infers natural rights from the duties it observes.[129] Reason cannot know the divine source of natural rights, but through the duties it knows the rights themselves as essential to the form and well-being of fallen life. But Bonhoeffer does not offer a more precise account of how unbelievers arrive at the same rights known to believers.

Bonhoeffer implies an answer in his notion of life. As we have seen life actively seeks its rights, dynamically asserting itself on their behalf. Bonhoeffer speaks of life "turning against" the unnatural and "bringing about" its downfall. "Life is its own physician", and "wards off" the unnatural offering "resistance" to its destructive forces. "The natural is the safeguarding of life against the unnatural and somehow sees to it that those injuring the natural "will suffer for it".[130] The natural possesses this power because it commands the assent and the approval of the "underlying will" of preserved life "which imbues the natural with it own inherent strength". For "life itself is on the side of the natural".[131]

Certain corollaries then follow. Life possesses a drive or desire for its own preservation and fulfillment. God works through the dynamic force of life on behalf of the natural and guarantees the preservation of natural rights.[132]  Bodily joys are not known as rights of natural life solely because one knows them to be a gift from God.  All persons acknowledge the rights of the body because life itself somehow conveys to the body its right to preservation and enjoyment.  "Bodily life," Bonhoeffer says,

> carries within itself the right to its own pres-
> ervation...it is in the strictest sense an 'innate'
> right, one which pre-exists our will, a right
> which rests upon the nature of things as
> they are.[133]

It could be said that God's desire for life[134] is imbedded in life itself. Life is then, in large part, an aggregate of desires for human joy and fulfillment, through which God constitutes life and gives it its force in its ongoing struggle against the unnatural.  This conclusion does not violate the text we have examined, but Bonhoeffer does not yet draw it.  Later in the Ethics, we will see him move in this direction. For now, he leaves unclear the manner in which reason assents to the rights of natural life.

In summary, Bonhoeffer's discussion of the natural and, in particular, his section on "The Right to Bodily Life" provide several illuminative connections to the provocative insights of the Letters and Papers from Prison.  Bonhoeffer's recognition of the rights to enjoyment of earthly life in the portions of the Ethics just analyzed could have been maintained within the harsh Reformation perspective on the Fall.  Human protection and enjoyment of earthly good would then have been simply evil and sinful.  God would permit the believer to pursue earthly joys merely because the pursuit was inescapable part of fallen life and necessary to His preservative ordering of the world.  God, in this perspective, would command spouses to eat, establish a home, and have sex with one another, but he would not command them to enjoy it.  He would tolerate, condone and grant the attendant pleasure only because it is inseparable from the eating, the home life and the sex itself.  The permission or the toleration of the Christian's enjoyment of earthly goods would remain, but neither the pursuit nor the enjoyment would contain in themselves anything truly and intrinsically good, worthwhile or beautiful.  The believer would not be encouraged to seek such enjoyment.

But Bonhoeffer does not cast his discussion in this light, as he did before 1939.  Now he insists that bodily life and the pleasures associated with it are gifts of God.  They are intrinsically valuable, and God wants Christians to seek and enjoy them as ends in themselves. Bonhoeffer still acknowledges the sinfulness of all dimensions of fallen earthly life. But he affirms that life enjoys rights, God's gifts to man. They must be taken seriously, respected and enjoyed in themselves, without reference to higher purpose. Elements of goodness and humanity are imbedded in the preserved life which should be sought and enjoyed for their own sake. These things remain penultimate in an absolute sense, an "empty jest" with respect to the ultimate, but they are still to be pursued as ends in themselves. This is why the rich young ruler, though lacking higher spiritual vision and purpose, is loved by Christ for his devotion to the good found in natural life.

By his very denial of all absolute value in the penultimate, Bonhoeffer forms the basis for the affirmation of its relative value. God gives good things of the earth to be enjoyed and loved for their intrinsic goodness, beauty and worth. Persons appropriately desire and relish them as ends in themselves, even when they do not perceive or acknowledge their divine giver. Bonhoeffer will stress these "good things" (Lebenswerte) of the earth in the Letters and Papers from Prison, their value (Werte), the happiness they afford, and their beauty.[135] But he does the groundwork for that assignation of value to secular realities in his discussion of the natural, and particularly in his remarks about God's gifts, rights to bodily life and its joys, the relative seriousness of the penultimate, and participation in the glory of creation.

In Chapter IV, Bonhoeffer breaks new ground in his understanding of earthly life. He begins to elucidate the relative independence of human love and the appropriateness of purely secular desires, affirmed later in the Letters. He urges Christians to live the natural life, for "this relative freedom is still important even for him to whom Christ has given the freedom for God and for his neighbour".[136] Inasmuch as they live naturally, believers do not refer to God at all, but live the natural life in and for itself. They are to know and will the natural life itself and nothing else. Inasmuch as they live naturally, believers do not know or will God's presence in creating, guiding or preserving their lives. Living naturally, the Christian also cannot know or will God's will as redemptive and moving human life toward its final goal. Insofar as they live natural life, Christians can will only natural life itself and live it for its own sake. They are to live natural life out of their fallen freedom and reason, and yet in doing so they will something which God also wills in His creative, conserving and redemptive willing.

The Christian does all of the above only insofar as he lives the natural life. For by faith, the Christian at the same time knows and wills the creative, preserving and redemptive purposes of God and seeks them wholeheartedly. Yet the life which God wills to create, preserve and redeem is falln earthly life. So, the Christian is called to live not only by faith, but also wholly in the natural life for its own sake. He thereby exists in the tension of God's "yes" and "no", living the fallen earthly life for its own sake, recognizing its status in the light of the ultimate, respecting this life and taking it seriously in its own right, and knowing in faith that it is God who wills this relative independence from His purposes. In essence, living the natural life means living as if there were no God, before God.

Chapter IV brings us closer to understanding the relative independence of human love in the life of the Christian as described in the Letters. The Christian lives natural life ultimately for Christ and His purposes, but he also lives it as an end it itself. This affirmation of natural life as both a means to an end and end in itself is fundamental to the encouragement which Bonhoeffer gives to Bethge in the Letters. For if the good things of natural life are to be sought and enjoyed as ends in themselves, it follows, although Bonhoeffer does not state in Chapter IV, that human desires for these joys would be justified and appropriate for the Christian without conscious reference to Christ. The Christian, in effect, knows the higher origins and purposes of life, but lives the natural life as fully and wholeheartedly as those who do not.

This represents a crucial movement in Bonhoeffer's thought. He now grants that bodily life and the pleasures associated with it are rightly to be understood as ends in themselves for all people. In his pre-1939 writings, Bonhoeffer also says that there is an intrinsic good or value in bodily joys; yet it remains unclear in what this good or value consists. Bonhoeffer implies that bodily joys are good because of what one experiences and consciously enjoys in them. He suggests it in the assertion that unbelievers know of this "value" or "goodness" by virtue of their reason and its ability to discern the "underlying will" of life. In essence, he says that there is something discernibly of value in the joys of the body which is known universally. All persons experience a happiness in such moments without conscious reference to God, and all experience something good or of value in that happiness.

But what good can there be in the experience? Only God is good. What is it in the desire or the pleasure sought that can be experienced as good without reference to God? How precisely does fallen reason know it to be good or of value?

Further, what is it, ontologically, in the reality itself which makes it good or valuable? Bonhoeffer gives a clue in the "the rights of natural life are...the reflected splendor of the glory of God's creation". Another clue is found in his remarks on life itself and its will towards the natural. But he has not gone far along these roads. In the continuing analysis of the Ethics, we will examine Bonhoeffer's attempts to elucidate further the dialectic he has established, with particular reference ot the questions central to our inquiry.

## V

In Chapter V, entitled "Christ, Reality and Good", Bonhoeffer casts more light upon the "goodness" of the things of earth and personal, secular longings for them. Bonhoeffer starts once more by insisting that Christ has rendered all two-realm thinking obsolete. Reality is now held in the tension wrought in the person of Christ. It remains fallen, evil, "disordered" and "under the power of the devil",[137] but reconciled in Christ Who calls believers to partake of that life and to seek the relative "goodness" in man and in the things of the earth.[138] Christ has structured reality so that Christians take part in the reality of the world and the reality of God simultaneously.[139] One cannot, therefore, speak of earth's good things without reference, knowingly or not, to the God Who has called them into being. Yet, as we saw in the preceding discussion of the natural and the rights of bodily life, the good things which persist in earthly life are experienced as valuable by all, whether they acknowledge the divine giver or not. The good in reality is accessible to man's experience and reason without the assistance of faith.

The questions we posed from the outset remain not fully answered. How can this experience or reasoning without God find its object good or valuable in itself? How does the knowledge of God confirm and assist the believer in living this good earthly life to the fullest? How can desires for the good things of the earth be encouraged and urged upon Christians when only God is good? We will now examine further Bonhoeffer's presentation of the relative value inherent in earthly reality and the good to be found in secular desires and the natural life without God.

As Bonhoeffer explains it, reality is one, the reality of God made "manifest in Christ in the reality of the world".[140] Christ has "encompassed, seized, and possessed" the world,[141] thereby reformulating the basic questions of ethics. Christian are no longer to ask themselves "How can I be good?", or "How can I do good?",[142] for the questions reveal a preoccupation with oneself and the world. Instead, believers are to strive that "the reality of God should show itself everywhere to be the ultimate reality".[143] This understanding of Christ's reconciliation of the world to Himself also brings an end to traditional two-realm thinking which offered persons an ill-conceived and insoluble dichotomy:

> So long as Christ and the world are conceived
> in two opposing and mutually repellent spheres,
> man will be left in the following dilemma:
> he abandons reality as a whole, and places
> himself in one or the other of the two spheres.
> He seeks Christ without the world, or he seeks
> the world without Christ.[144]

A third choice is somehow to seek both and become "the man of eternal conflict".[145] Bonhoeffer believed this third option to be most perplexing to the modern Christian and was committed to its elimination:

> It may be difficult to break the spell of
> this thinking in terms of two spheres, but it
> is nevertheless quite certain that it is in
> profound contradiction to the thought of the
> Bible and to the thought of the Reformation,
> and that consequently it aims wide of reality.
> There are not two realities, but only one re-
> ality, and that is the reality of God, which has
> become manifest in Christ in the reality of
> the world. Sharing in Christ we stand at once
> in both the reality of God and the reality of
> the world. The reality of Christ comprises
> the reality of the world within itself. The world
> has no reality of its own, independently of
> the revelation of God in Christ. One is denying
> the revelation of God in Jesus Christ if one
> tries to be "Christian" without seeing and
> recognizing the world in Christ.[146]

Bonhoeffer suggests that in the two-realm scheme good was to be sought outside of earthly realities, thereby cutting off the Christian from the world. Those who devoted themselves to the world and its values were said to abandon the way of God and became pawns of Satan. Through His reconciliation, Christ has resolved this conflict and made it possible for the believer to live fully in the world and in God at the same time.

This does not mean that the world's status as "forlorn" and "godless" has been changed; it remains fallen, yet simultaneously reconciled and claimed by God. Christ has resolved the two-realm dilemma by establishing an interdependence between the Christian and secular elements of the Christian's life.

> A world which stands by itself, in isolation
> from the law of Christ, falls victim to license
> and self-will. A Christianity which withdraws
> from the world falls victim to the unnatural
> and the irrational, to presumption and self-
> will.
> Ethical thinking in terms of spheres, then,
> is invalidated by faith in the revelation of the
> ultimate reality in Jesus Christ, and this
> means that there is no real possibility of being
> a Christian outside the reality of the world and
> that there is no real worldly existence outside
> the reality of Jesus Christ.[147]

In Christ, as we have seen, the "world, the natural, the profane and reason are all taken up into God from the outset",[148] and find a unity in Him. Each bears witness to the other of their union. Each requires the presence of the other lest it distort the balance upon which earthly reality depends.

Bonhoeffer, then, offers two arguments for living a full earthly life. The first, which re-states the argument of Chapter IV, is that such a life is natural and intended by God for all persons.[149] The failure to lead such a life is unnatural and harmful to that structured reality. The second argument is new to the Ethics. Bonhoeffer insists that the secular has a right, indeed a duty, to admonish and correct the Church when it misrepresents itself and the secular. This duty of the secular to act as a corrective for the Church implies a certain goodness in the fallen world, for it suggests that the secular possesses values which it must insist the Church respect.

When, therefore, the Church withdraws from the world, the secular demands that it return to its calling as a partner in the historical process. It reminds the Church of the earthly values which it is called to support. Likewise, when the secular rejects the law of Christ which gives it form, it is the Church which must insist that a genuine secularity be restored and that earthly values be re-established. In both cases, Christ is proclaimed as the only reality, whether those taking part in the process realize it or not.[150]

Good, therefore, is not to be found in sorting out the godly from the ungodly elements in the midst of fallen reality. The Christian is to live fully in the one reality reconciled in Christ, and therein do the good of God:

> The question of good becomes the question of
> participation in the divine reality which is
> revealed in Christ... The wish to be good con-
> sists solely in the longing for what is real in
> God... Good is not a correspondence between a
> criterion which is placed at our disposal by
> nature or whatever entity I may designate as
> reality. Good is reality itself, reality seen
> and recognized in God... Participation in the
> indivisible whole of the divine reality - this
> is the sense and the purpose of the Christian
> enquiry concerning good.[151]

But how can participation in fallen, ungodly, wicked reality, albeit reconciled reality, be good and urged upon the Christian? Earthly wickedness perpetually opposes the Church and the Kingdom of Christ. How can Bonhoeffer encourage the Christian to participate fully in a world which remains "disordered"[152] and contrary to Christ?

These questions take us to the heart of Bonhoeffer's thought in Chapter V. The world persists in opposing, resisting, and rejecting the reality of God's love in Jesus Christ,[153] yet it has been reconciled to God "whether it recognizes it or not".[154] The Church acknowl- edges, although the world does not, that even in its godlessness "it is solely and entirely the world of Christ".[155] This knowledge, Bonhoef- fer argues, is the only distinguishing feature between the believing and unbelieving communities:

> The Church it divided from the world solely by
> the fact that she affirms in faith the reality
> of God's acceptance of man, a reality which is
> the property of the whole world.[156]

As a believing member of the Church, the Christian lives the earthly life as fully as the non-Christian. But only the Christian af- firms the reconciliation through which Christ claims that fallen re- ality as His own. In essence, the Christian lives in conflict. He af- firms the world which crucified Christ and encourages himself to enjoy those good things of the earth which, in their fallenness, reject and resist His Lordship. But now the conflict is a conflict-in-unity and not the "eternal conflict" usually associated with two-realm thinking.

Still, our questions remain. Why should Bonhoeffer encourage the believer to live the fallen earthly life to the fullest? Bonhoeffer states the opposition between fallen reality and God's reconciling love more strongly than ever before; it "opposes', "resists", and is "engaged in a life and death struggle with the Church".[157] Yet he also offers his most powerful statement thus far on earthly values in his discussion of the mandates.

Labor, marriage, government and the Church all result from the Fall, and yet all are divinely imposed tasks, each in "its own way... through Christ, directed towards Christ, and in Christ".[158] The mandates are not divine in themselves, but are divine insofar as they are a part of God's preservative purpose. Further, these mandates are imposed not only upon Christians, but upon all persons so there can be no retreat from a "secular" into a "spiritual sphere".[159] Despite their fallen character, Bonhoeffer affirms for the first time here the human creation of value in the concrete forms of the mandates of labor and marriage. Man can create values himself.[160] Through labor, for example, persons participate in the action of creation. By their labor Christians build and experience "that likeness of the celestial world by which the man who recognizes Jesus Christ is reminded of the Lost Paradise". Labor has a "general usefulness" and value, for through labor "a world of things and values" is created which is designed to serve Jesus Christ, but which serves man in the penultimate as well.[161] Labor produces instruments of music whose lovely sounds yield a foretaste of the symphony in heaven for the believer, being already lovely in themselves and valued as such. The extraction and processing of precious metals from the earth remind the believer of the priceless treasures which willfill the realm of heaven. But these metals also serve to beautify earthly homes and may become instruments of defense and justice to protect the values of earth.[162]

A similar creation of values takes place in marriage. In marriage, too, believers take part in the on-going process of creation, sharing in God's plan to perpetuate life and increase His kingdom.[163] Christians recognize the divine task of educating their children to be obedient to Christ that His objectives on earth may be served. The producing and raising of children is a creative process in which believers and non-believers participate through marriage.

New persons are created, and with them the values associated with personhood, all within the framework of a mandate tainted by the Fall. As Bonhoeffer reminds us, the first son of the first man was a murderer, which casts a perpetual shadow over the joys of marriage and family.

This affirmation of man's cretion of values in his fallen, earthly life is a major movement ahead in Bonhoeffer's thought. He had argued in Chapter IV that the natural life enjoys rights which are given by God and reflect the glory of His creation. He implied their intrinsic value as gifts of a gracious donor. Now he asserts that man in his fallen freedom is able to produce values in natural life, thereby participating in God's on-going creation. This is a far bolder endorsement of value in the natural than Bonhoeffer expressed in Chapter IV. As we have begun to see in Chapter V and will see further in what follows, Bonhoeffer's willingness to speak of value in fallen, earthly life is a major step further in explaining his encouragement of the Christian to desire the earth's good things for their own sake.

The mandates, therefore, are both fallen and value-producing, sinful "in themselves" and yet creative of earthly good. This real conflict is kept but reconciled in Christ such that full participation in the mandates is the only way to enjoy unity in one's concrete life and action:

> The whole man stands before the whole earthly and eternal reality, the reality which God has prepared for him in Jesus Christ. Man can live up to this reality only if he responds fully to the totality of the offer and the claim. The first three mandates are not designed to divide man up, to tear asunder; they are concerned with the whole man before God, the Creator, Reconciler and Redeemer; reality, therefore, in all its multiplicity is ultimately one; it is one in the incarnate God Jesus Christ, and precisely this is the testimony which the Church must give. The divine mandates in the world are not intended to consume man in endless conflicts; on the contrary, they are directed toward the whole man, as he stands in reality before God.[164]

To summarize: Bonhoeffer makes several new assertions in Chapter V which are central to our inquiry. He affirms once again the tension which inheres its reconciled earthly life, namely, that

106

Christ accepts reality in its fallenness, its evil and its opposition to His purposes. He had already affirmed this in Chapter III, but he now describes and develops this tension in more detail. The believer, like his Lord, is to accept that earthly life and live it fully; moreover, the secular rightly corrects the Church when it fails to uphold earthly values. Furthermore, that "disordered", fallen life creates values itself. Bonhoeffer thereby develops the dynamic notion of earthly life introduced in Chapter IV. Here, the "underlying will" of life is manifested in the creation of values which enhance and preserve fallen life. Bonhoeffer condemns earthly reality as strongly as ever, but also affirms its value more profoundly than before. These positive developments in Bonhoeffer's appraisal of natural life are major progressions in his encouragement to the believer to desire and to enjoy the good things of the earth for their own sake.

## VI

Almost immediately upon completing Chapter V in the summer of 1941, Bonhoeffer began work on the succeeding chapter, "History and the Good", which he finished by April of 1942. Bonhoeffer elaborates here the dialectic between God as the only source of good and godless earthly realities as relatively good. He develops the ways in which these real opposites are united in Christ. In one sense, Christ is life itself for the Christian,[165] yet His "yes" and "no" to the earth and the believer's responsibility through pertinence (Sachgemässheit) to earthly realities provide a framework in which the believer also can and should devote himself wholeheartedly to earthly life and to its good things for their own sake. The Christian, therefore, lives in Christ and in relative independence from Him and His purposes. Bonhoeffer implies that, although the Christian lives in and through Christ in an absolute sense, life in relative abstraction from Christ is worth living in itself. The problem with this claim, as we have stressed from the outset, is how one can experience the good in life and desire it for its own sake, if Christ is the only good and the essence of life itself. Further, how can Christian faith promote such a movement back into earthly life and its good things? In what follows, we will see how Bonhoeffer develops his view of earthly life and approaches an answer to our questions.

Bonhoeffer repeats what he explained in Chapter V: the Christian acknowledges the unity of God and world effected through Christ, and therefore no longer perceives life as a battleground of two competing realities. Instead, he sees a single, if bipolar reality, reconciled in Christ and drawn into His purposes. As a result, the believer never knows good and evil in their pure form, for they do not exist as such,[166] but only as they make themselves known in daily, believing life. Christian faith alone, therefore, yields knowledge of the good. It is unwarranted to seek the good in the abstract and not in Christ. To find the good, one must look into life itself and discover that which good for living persons in the one reality united in Christ.[167]

As the Christian looks into life, however, he confronts the tension of judgment and reconciliation which inheres in preserved life. The recognition that Jesus Christ is life itself immediately condemns and negates one's life, for it places into bold relief the fact that life is no longer one's own:

> My life is outside myself, outside the range of
> my disposal; my life is another than myself;
> it is Jesus Christ... "I am the life". This is
> the word, the revelation, the proclamation of
> Jesus Christ...This word is addressed to us,
> and when we hear it we recognize that we
> have fallen away from life, from our life, and
> that we are living in contradiction to life, to
> our life. In this saying of Jesus Christ, there-
> fore, we hear the condemnation, the negation,
> of our life; for our life is not life; or, if it is
> life, it is life only by virtue of the fact that,
> even though in contradiction to it, we still
> live through the life which is called Jesus
> Christ, the origin, the essence and the goal of
> all life and or our life.[168]

Bonhoeffer's "condemnation" and "negation" of earthly life is the translator's rendering of a simple "Nein!" in the German text. This "no" means essentially that the life we live, meaning our fallen, earthly life, is not our real life but cut off from real life which is Christ, and lived in contradiction to that life. Life persists only because Christ has reconciled it in his death and resurrection. He reigns as Lord of fallen life. This "no" to fallen life is a reminder that death, both Christ's and our own, stands between man and the life which is Jesus Christ. Man's apostasy has resulted in annihilation, crucifixion, judgment and condemnation.[169]

Yet, in the face of this "no", Christ returns to life to man with an emphatic "yes". This "yes" affirms Christ's gifts to man of rec-onciled life in Himself:

> ...in bringing us death this "no" brings a mys-

terious "yes", the affirmation of a new life,
the life which is Jesus Christ. This is the
life which we cannot give ourselves, the life
that comes to us entirely from without, entirely from beyond; and yet it is not a remote
or alien life, or no concern to ourselves, but it
is our own real daily life.[170]

The daily existence of man in only fully understood through
this dialectic of Christ. The "yes" speaks of creation, reconciliation
and redemption. It affirms that life is given to man in Christ and
that it has its origin, its essence and its goal only in Him. The "no" is
the rejection of a life fallen from its origin, essence and goal. It
rejects and condemns, sentencing to death a life torn free from its
source.

The "no" and the "yes" are intimately interrelated, just as
Christ's crucifixion and resurrection. Bonhoeffer argues, as he had
earlier,[171] that the "no" and the "yes" mutually embrace all of life, at
once endorsing and denying it, setting it free and binding it, yet ever
uniting life in the person of Jesus Christ in Whom and through
Whom life persists. Bonhoeffer describes at length and in detail this
inherent tension of human life:

It is the "yes" to what is created, to becoming
and to growth, to the flower and to the fruit,
to health, happiness, ability, achievement,
worth, success, greatness and honour; in
short, it is the "yes" to the development of
the power of life. And it is the "no" to that
defection from the origin, the essence and the
goal of life which is inherent in all this existence from the outset. This "no" means
dying, suffering, poverty, renunciation,
resignation, humility, degradation, self-
denial, and in this again it already implies the
"yes" to the new life, a life which does not
fall apart into a juxtaposition of "yes" and
"no", a life in which there is not to be found,
for example, an unrestrained expansion of vitality side by side with a wholly separate ascetic and spiritual attitude, or "creaturely"
conduct side by side with "Christian" conduct.
If that were so, the "yes" and the "no" would
lose their unity in Jesus Christ; it is in tension between the "yes" and the "no" in the

sense that in every "yes" the "no is already
heard and in every "no there is heard also
the "yes". Development of the vital force
and self-denial, growing and dying, health
and suffering, happiness and renunciation,
achievement and humility, honour and self-
abasement, all these belong together in irreconcilable contradiction and yet in living
unity.[172]

The believer must know the unity which this tension brings to his
way of life. If the "no" is separated from the "yes", an abstract ethic
of vitality or an ascetic, pseudoethic of Jesus will result and destroy
life's intrinsic unity in Christ.[173] The life which the Christian is
encouraged to live is a life torn free from its source, in certain
respects relatively free of Christ in its fallenness, and condemned for
that reason. It is a life which opposes Christ, resists Him, is in "contradiction" to Him, a life to which He says "no". Yet it is returned by
His reconciliation to the Christian to be lived fully. Only in living this
earthly life wholly under the "yes" and "no" of God can the believer
live genuinely out of his faith. The Christian is not placed in the
position of having to choose the "secular" or "Christian" path for
himself; instead, he lives in the fullness of life reconciled in Christ
and united in the tension of His person.[174]

Bonhoeffer's examples clarify the tension of the "yes" and
"no" out of which the believer lives. The Christian hears God's "yes"
to earthly happiness, an affirmation in which God urges earthly joy
upon His people. This is not merely a "yes" of permission, but a
"yes" of encouragement, a distinct affirmation of earthly life and its
good things. Nowhere else before 1939 nor earlier in the Ethics does
Bonhoeffer so unambiguously claim that God urges the believer to
seek out earthly happiness. God's "yes" is accompanied by the "no"
of renunciation, in which the Christian is reminded, as he was in
Chapter IV, that the good things of the earth are fallen, condemned,
an "empty jest" in the presence of the ultimate. But the "no" does not
annul the "yes", nor does the "yes" invalidate the "no". The unceasing declaration of both "yes" and "no" comprise the inherent contradiction which Christ's reconciliation imposes upon fallen, earthly
life.

This abiding contradiction emerges in Bonhoeffer's account of
Christian vocation. Christ Himself calls the believer to earthly
duties, but at the same time negates that calling in the midst of His
summons:

This call does indeed summon him to earthly
duties, but that is never the whole of the call,
for it lies always beyond these duties, before
them and behind them. The calling, in the New
Testament sense, is never a sanctioning of
worldly institutions as such; its "yes" to
them always includes at the same time and extremely emphatic "no", an extremely sharp
protest against the world. Luther's return
from the monastery to the world, to the
"calling", is, in the true New Testament sense,
the fiercest attack and assault to be launched
against the world since primitive Christianity.
Now a man takes up his position against
the world in the world; the calling is the place
at which the call of Christ is answered, the
place at which a man lives responsibly.[175]

The "yes" and the "no" therefore establish the believer's daily station
in the world over against the world.

The Christian, then, lives in the unity of the contradiction of
Christ's "yes" and "no":

...in selfless self-assertion, in self-assertion
in the sacrifice of ourselves to God and to
men... The life which confronts us in Jesus
Christ... requires the response of a life
which assimilates and unites this 'yes'
and this'no'.[176]

The call to "selfless self-assertion" epitomizes this contradiction in
that selflessness represents the believer's recognition of life's
fallenness and ultimate reliance upon Christ; it is the "no" to one's
self and the disordered world. Self-assertion, on the other hand,
echoes the "yes" to created life, to its relative freedom from God and
for oneself as grasped in the Fall.

Christ commands both selflessness and self-assertion in the
life which He urges and reconciles. Such a life demonstrates Christian responsibility and issues forth in "deputyship", or the "complete
surrender of one's own life to the other man".[177] The believer, like
Christ, is to concern himself with the welfare of others and devote
himself entirely to the community of persons of which he is a part.

111

Living reconciled life means bearing the responsibility for others which a natural life implies. It is in living the natural earthly life, in its relative independence from Christ, that one freely assumes responsibilities for others and builds the network of duties which give form to his life:

> The structure of responsible life is con-
> ditioned by two factors; life is bound to man
> and to God and a man's own life is free. It is
> the fact that life is bound to man and to God
> which sets life in the freedom of a man's own
> life. Without this bond and without this free-
> dom there is no responsibility. Only when it
> has become selfless in this obligation does a
> life stand in the freedom of a man's truly own
> life and action.[178]

This notion of responsibility in deputyship in response to the "yes" and "no" of Christ was certainly at the heart of Bonhoeffer's decision to sacrifice himself for the sake of the German people and their civilization.

But responsible living extends beyond the relation of persons to other persons. It also includes the believer's responsibility for things and for the relative values of the earth:

> Through Christ the world of things and of val-
> ues is once more directed towards mankind as
> it was in the Creation. It is only within these
> limits that there is a legitimate sense in
> speaking, as is often done, about responsi-
> bility for a thing or for a cause... There is a
> devotion to the cause of truth, goodness,
> justice and beauty which would be profaned if
> one were to ask what is the use of it, and
> which indeed makes it abundantly clear
> that the highest values must be subservient
> to man.[179]

The devoting of oneself to earthly values, to the truth, goodness, justice and beauty experienced by all, is a worthy enterprise for the Christian without his referring to any higher purpose. Any inquiry into the purpose or "use" of this devotion profanes it. Bonhoeffer, of course, is rejecting Nazism and its subordination of all earthly values to its cause. Single-minded involvement with the thing or value as an end in itself reflects its essential value to man, and in fact also serves higher purposes.

It is this devotion to earthly realities, to the domain of things, which Bonhoeffer calls "pertinence". There are two facets of a pertinent attitude. The first is an awareness of the extensive relation of things to God and man:

> ...that attitude to things is pertinent which
> keeps steadily in view their original, essen-
> tial and purposive relation to God and to men.
> This relation does not corrupt them in their
> character as things, but it purifies this char-
> acter; it does not extinguish the ardour of
> devotion to a cause, but it refines and intensi-
> fies it. The greater the purity of the service
> to a cause or to a thing, and the more com-
> pletely this service is free from personal sub-
> sidiary aims, the more thoroughly the thing
> itself will recover its original relation to
> God and to man, and the more completely
> it will set man free from himself.[180]

Pertinence, therefore, enables the believer to live both without God, and yet with God. Bonhoeffer goes on to say that a pertinent attitude also enables a man to find himself and to be served by the thing. As he explains:

> If, for example, an attempt is made to render
> a science useful to men in an illegitimately
> direct manner for demagogic, pedagogic or
> moralistic purposes, then it is not only the
> man but also the science which is ruined. If,
> on the other hand, in this science man exclu-
> sively and unreservedly serves the cause of
> truth, then in the selfless surrender of all his
> own wishes he finds himself and the thing for
> the sake of which he has rendered this self-
> less service must in the end serve him.[181]

The discerning of this original relation of things to Christ sets things free to be more fully themselves, and frees the person who serves them to be more fully human and more fully himself. The parallel to the cantus firmus is unmistakable here. Earthly values, things, and themes are able to develop to their "full sound", to borrow the imagery of the Letters and Papers from Prison, because the Christian is firmly rooted in his love for God and is able to allow earthly life to develop its myriad counterpoints. In some manner, knowing of Christ assists the believer in knowing of the essential relation of things to persons which, in turn, enables Christians to commit themselves to earthly values and causes so that they might attain the truth, beauty or good which is inherently their own.

The discussion of pertinence is relevant to our inquiry for several reasons. First, it establishes the world of "things" as ultimately reliant upon Christ for its purpose and its existence. Through faith, the believer can discern the original relation of things to God and, through his devotion to fallen, earthly realities, can enable them to develop as intended, fully and appropriately. The believer's service to the things of the earth, therefore, advances both the earthly reality itself and the purposes of God. In this devotion to the earth, the Christian lives fully in the domain of things, independent of any reference to God, though he knows in faith that God has given order to this reality and that it ultimately depends up Him.

The believer is also aware of the contradiction inherent in God's encouragement to such a life. For along with the "yes" to what is created and preserved, the Christian hears God's equally resounding "no" to earthly reality as fallen, judged and condemned for its opposition to His purposes. The world to which the Christian is called to devote himself is, at the same time, the world which has defected from its origin and exists in contradiction to the person and work of Christ.

We have here, then, in the midst of the "yes" and the "no", in the call to happiness and to renunciation, and in the summons to Christian vocation in the world, a call to full participation in life itself. If persons live responsibly within life's contradiction, hindrances to such a way of life will produce yearnings for the experience of things once enjoyed and now missed, or not yet not enjoyed. In short, a Christian devotion to the domain of things naturally generates longings for the good things of the earth. Bonhoeffer does not explicitly draw this conclusion here, but it is a natural connection between this portion of the Ethics and the later affirmation of earthly desires in the Letters and Papers from Prison.

The discussion of pertinence and the relative independence of earthly values and things does not alter the fact that Christ remains the essence of life for the Christian. But earthly life is, in some sense, relatively meaningful in itself, although broadly encompassed in the person and purposes of Christ. The believer's faith helps him to see the original purpose of things and to serve them freely and devotedly. Through this devotion, made possible by faith, life's good things develop toward their intended form, to the benefit of earthly life and to all persons. The relationship of faith to the believer's wholehearted devotion to earthly life corresponds to the cantus firmus and the relative independence of the counterpoints. In this chapter, Bonhoeffer's extended account of Christ's "yes" and "no" to earthly life, his discussions of vocation and pertinence, and his implicit affirmation of the meaning of earthly life in relative distinction from Jesus Christ draw us nearer to his later encouragement of secular desires for life's good things for their own sake.

## VII

The final chapter of the Ethics, "The 'Ethical' and the 'Christian' as a Theme",[182] clarifies further what Bonhoeffer thought about earthly desires and the nature of earthly life. Having equated responsible living through deputyship with the Christian way of life in Chapter VI, Bonhoeffer begins, six months later, to inquire into the meaning of this for ethics and for the broader conception of life itself. In tone and substance, this chapter has the greatest affinity with the Letters and Papers from Prison, and throws considerable light upon the issues under our consideration. But it does not, as we shall later argue, resolve all the difficulties which attend Bonhoeffer's account of earthly desires and the Christian's life without God.

Bonhoeffer first raises the question of the place and form in which ethics are to be a part of the Christian life, and his conclusions are startling. The place of ethics has been exaggerated in the past, leading persons to believe that, at every moment, ethical decisions of import must be made. In actuality, this is only rarely the case. Ethics is not at the core of life, perpetually engaging persons in the task of distinguishing good from evil. Rather, ethics is on the edge of human life, from where it can make a contribution when called upon, but normally does not interfere with everyday life:

> Certainly there is a necessary time and place
> in human existence for the so-called 'ethical
> phenomenon', that is to say, the experience of
> obligation, the conscious and deliberate
> decision between something which is, on
> principle, evil, the ordering of life in accor-
> dance with a supreme standard, moral con-
> flict and moral resolve. One may, therefore,
> suppose that within these limits it can and
> should be made a theme for discussion. But
> precisely this proper delimiting of the place
> and of the time is of crucial importance if one

is to prevent a pathological overburdening of
life by the ethical... To confine the ethical
phenomenon to its proper place and time is
not to invalidate it; it is, on the contrary, to
render it fully operative.[183]

The danger of elevating ethics into the forefront of life is that it
binds life to a method where none is needed. "Should" is to be heard
only in extreme circumstances. When it becomes a recurring them,
the result is a "pedantic regimentation of the whole of life".[184] When
ethics establishes a set of abstract principles to be followed scrupulously, life is reduced to a "bleak and monotonous uniformity", and
an alien structure is imposed upon it.[185] When relegated to its
proper place on the periphery, ethics sets limits which protect the
fullness and freedom of life at whose edge it stands.

When Bonhoeffer describes life, he consistently writes of its
spontaneity and free-flowing character. It is a "vital process", moved
forward by an abundance of motives, of which persons are only partly
aware.[186] It is a process in which persons take part naturally,
almost unconsciously. The ethical, with its rules and requirements,
does not fit such a life. With ethics establishing its parameters, life
can freely flow its way without interruption. It moves ahead as a
"vital process" in which persons are released from the ethical for
"unreflected doing".[187] The ethical, for the most part, is a spectator
to the unfolding abundance of life:

In respect to its contents as well as its character as an experience the ethical phenomenon
is a peripheral event. 'Shall' and 'should', both
as contents and as experience, are appropriate
to a situation in which something is not,
either because it cannot be or else because it
is not desired.[188]

This last sentence suggests a profound truth about the nature
of life. From within the boundaries of the ethical, life is determined
by a multiplicity of human desires experienced by persons without
recourse to ethical deliberation. The ethical has a voice only when
something is not. the ethical speaks a "no" or a "should not" when
the natural fellowship of a family, a marriage, or of the organization
in which one works is threatened. That which is harmful to the
freely desired natural life is repelled by the ethical, which directs
persons to desire once more the joys of natural life. All of life would
suffer were the ethical to permit such things to continue. The natu-

ral would be damaged and the "underlying will" of life, discussed in Chapter IV, would be thwarted.[189] The ethical is thus a defender of preserved life when its well-being is threatened. Bonhoeffer goes on to say that things which are not are not desired, thereby implying that things which are, persist in life because they are desired. As life runs its natural course, its "good" things are desired and enjoyed. This is the flow of life and the natural human response to it.

This complex notion of life is at the center of Bonhoeffer's perspective on earthly desires. Natural, earthly desires are vital, for they generate life's flow and lead to the development of other elements of life. In what follows Bonhoeffer develops this suggestion.

Since life's nature is to flow unhindered, all that is required of persons in the non-ethical process is to live freely and to do what is self-evident. As Bonhoeffer explains:

> My living in the fellowship of a family, a
> marriage, and of the organization in which I
> work and own property is primarily an obli-
> gation in which I acquiesce freely and one in
> which the 'ethical phenomenon', the objective
> and subjective aspects of 'shall' and 'should',
> does not come to light but remains dormant.[190]

Life in one's family, marriage and occupation is not an ethical task assigned from without, but a "good" in life which persons desire freely and naturally. It is not a duty imposed upon the individual, but arises from within as persons become a part of life's flow.[191]

As we have seen, natural life is formed concretely in the man-dates. When persons experience the natural and its "good" things, they desire to partake more fully in earthly life and "acquiesce freely" in life's flow. The ethical stands apart, both protecting and freely desired natural life, and encouraging full participation in that life.

> Ethics and ethicists do not intervene contin-
> uously in life...but, precisely by speaking
> strictly form the standpoint of the 'ethical';
> they wish to help people to learn to share in
> life without the limits of the obligation of
> 'shall' and 'should', and not hold themselves
> aloof from the processes of life as spec-
> tators, critics and judges; to share in life not
> out of the motive of 'shall' and 'should'. but

from the full abundance of vital motives;
from the natural and the organic, and from
free acceptance and will...[192]

Ethics protects life's flow, serving as a sentry on guard against the unnatural and the destructive. The flow of earthly desires enriches human life, helping persons to share in all dimensions of the natural life, while essentially unaware of the ethical. When life is at its best or most natural, the ethical is unnoticed.[193]

Having located ethics at the edge of human life, Bonhoeffer now argues that the only warrant for ethical discourse is the commandment of God.[194] This commandment comes in the person of Jesus Christ, takes from in the mandates of the Church, family, labor and government, and sets persons free to live in the abundance of that given life. It does not call persons out of life, but into it; it is a command to live unreservedly in the midst of life's flow. Unlike the "ethical", it stands at the center of human life:

> God's commandment, revealed in Jesus Christ,
> embraces the whole of life. It does not only,
> like the ethical, keep watch on the untrans-
> gressible frontier of life, but it is at the
> same time the centre and fullness of life. It
> is not only obligation but also permission. It
> does not only forbid, but it also sets free for
> life; it sets free for unreflected doing. It
> does not only interrupt the process of life
> when this process goes astray, but it guides
> and conducts this process even though there
> is not always need for consciousness of this
> fact. God's commandment becomes the daily
> divine guidance of our lives... through the
> commandment life does not fall apart into
> countless new beginnings, but it is given a
> clear direction, an inner continuity and a firm
> security. The commandment of God becomes
> the element in which one lives without
> always being conscious of it, and, thus it
> implies freedom of movement and of action,
> freedom from the fear of decision, freedom
> from fear to act, it implies certainty, quietude,
> confidence, balance and peace.[195]

The commandment of God is strikingly reminiscent of the

cantus firmus. While Bonhoeffer does not yet employ his musical metaphor, the similarity in function of the two is virtually identical. God's commandment is the underlying theme which sets free the other themes of the Christian's life to develop confidently and in "balance". One lives "without always being conscious of" the commandment, and yet is enabled by it to live the other dimensions of his natural life to the fullest. The parallel to the cantus firmus is even more conspicuous when Bonhoeffer speaks of the relationship of the commandment of God to the mandates:

> The commandment of Jesus Christ does indeed rule over Church, family, culture and government; but it does so while at the same time setting each of these mandates free for the fulfillment of its own allotted functions. Jesus Christ's claim to lordship, which is proclaimed by the Church, means at the same time the emancipation of family, culture and government for the realization of their own essential character which has its foundation in Christ.[196]

As Bonhoeffer adds in a footnote, "The antimony of heteronomy and autonomy is here resolved in a higher unity which we may call Christonomy".[197] Later, in the Letters, he will refer to this unity as a polyphony, or multi-dimensional life of Christ, but the meaning will be the same.

In addition, Bonhoeffer often insists that the commandment of God enables one to live without conscious reference to its presence and permission. The believer lives, in effect, under the commandment but without it. This sets him free for "unreflected doing", or living the natural life in relative abstraction from Jesus Christ and His purposes. We have here, then, a further reference to the "relative independence" of contrapuntal themes, and a clear statement, though less dramatically put, of Bonhoeffer's later call in the Letters for a life without God before God.

Unlike the ethical, which produces incessant self-scrutiny and moral anxiety with respect to one's motives and actions, the commandment of God brings confidence and inner peace. With its guidance the commandment releases the believer to live natural, earthly life without moral insecurity, free of the conflicts which were discussed in Chapter V. Over and over, Bonhoeffer writes of the certainty, the "clear direction", "inner continuity" and "firm security" which the Christian enjoys in the permission granted him to live fully.[198] Bonhoeffer's own concern for peace of mind and certitude is painfully evident in these pages as he seeks to justify the decisions he has made in his own life. Perhaps the overriding concern which prompted him to insist upon the "certainty, quietude, confidence, balance and peace" afforded by the commandment of God was his own very real struggle for these qualities in himself as he moved more deeply into the Resistance. The confidence he needed to support his commitment to the underground was not sufficiently engendered by traditional Lutheran perspectives on earthly life. The freedom and certitude granted by the commandment of God perhaps gave him the assurance he needed.

This marked contrast between the ethical and the life formed and set free in Christ is discussed by Bonhoeffer at length. The way of life promoted by the commandment is alien to a style of life restricted to the ethical. Disdaining the uniform principles for action characteristic of the ethical, the commandment of God encourages persons to trust in living and to live naturally out of desires and yearnings, unconsciously taking part in life's flow. Such a life is foreign and incomprehensible to the ethical:

> The 'ethical' is repelled and horrified by the obscurity of the motives for action, by the way in which every deed is compounded of conscious and unconscious elements, natural and supernatural elements, inclination and duty, egotism and altruism, volition and compulsion, activity and passivity, so that all doing is at the same time passive undergoing and vice versa.[199]

Simply put, the commandment of God lets persons live. Eating, sleeping, working, playing, resting and the like are all to be enjoyed without ethical reflection and introspection.[200] Wherever the mandates and the rights of bodily life are operative, which is virtually everywhere in life, persons are generally unaware of the ethical and urged to take part freely in the flow which is claimed, seized and set free by the divine commandment. Bonhoeffer summarizes his thoughts on life in quoting the verses of Matthias Claudius in a poem entitled "Man":

> Conceived and nursed by woman wondrously,
> He comes, sees, hears, is easily deceived.
> He hankers, craves, and sheds the tear that's
>     due,

120

Scorns and reveres, knows joy, knows danger,
    too,
Believes and doubts, errs, teaches, builds,
    destroys,
Torments himself with telling truth from
    falsehood.
He sleeps and watches, grows and eats and
    drinks.
His hair is one year brown, another grey.
And, if he lives so long, when four-score
    years
Are done he lays himself beside his fathers
And never comes again.[201]

    This poem depicts the life of which the ethical "knows nothing".[202] It is a life characterized by hopes, desires, dreams and cravings, by disappointments, fears, promises unfulfilled and tears, yet if flows on richly and abundantly. Life is very much desires, satisfied and unsatisfied, desires for the "good" things which are a part of life. All persons, as we have seen, experience the value of the mandates and of bodily joys. Without access to their Source, persons still desire the constitutive elements of life, and thus life itself. Their existence is in great part a composite of desires for the innumerable "goods" of the world put into place by a gracious God.

    In Chapter VII, Bonhoeffer draws together many of the themes which we have seen develop through the Ethics and joins them with the radical statements of the Letters. Specifically, his exposition of the natural life, as fully pursued and enjoyed by the Christian under the commandment of God, casts considerable light upon the cantus firmus and the contrapuntal dimension of human, earthly life. This life, though fallen, godless, wicked and relatively independent of Christ, is the life in which the Christian participates with an easy conscience unburdened by perpetual moral anxiety. The believer lives as if there were no God in a world which does not know Him, in certitude that the command of Christ encourages and urges that life. In becoming a part of life's flow, the Christian enables fallen life to develop its full independence and, at the same time, allows it "to be what it really is before God, namely, a world which in its godlessness is reconciled with God".[203] Living the full natural life under the commandment of God not only enhances that life itself, but enhances the humanness of the believer as well. Only when persons live such "genuine worldliness" can the fallen world, the Christian himself, and the purposes of God be fulfilled.

But does this bold conception of life satisfactorily tie together the difficulties we observed in the <u>Letters</u> <u>and</u> <u>Papers</u> <u>from</u> <u>Prison</u>? Does it coherently answer all the questions which we posed at the outset? In the chapter which follows, our conclusion, we will attempt to fit together the fragments we have analyzed through the <u>Ethics</u> into a complete account of Bonhoeffer's view of life without God and of desires for the "good" things of the earth for their own sake. After bringing together as best we can what Bonhoeffer intended, we will ask whether his thoughts present a cohesive account of the meaning of human life and Christian devotion to the things of the earth, remain unsuited for systematic arrangement, or whether they fail to present a cohesive account and yet seem suited, nevertheless, for ultimate systematic arrangement.

## Notes to Chapter III

[1] This point is brought out clearly by John Godsey in his working paper "Bonhoeffer's Doctrine of Love", presented to The International Bonhoeffer Society meeting in San Francisco in December of 1981. Godsey refers specifically to a lecture delivered by Bonhoeffer in November of 1932 on "Thy Kingdom Come! The Prayer of the Church for God's Kingdom on Earth" in which he wrote: "Whoever loves God... loves him as Lord of the earth as it is; and whoever loves the earth loves it as God's earth. Whoever loves God's kingdom, loves it wholly as God's kingdom, but he also loves it as God's kingdom on earth" ("Thy Kingdom Come!." translated in John D. Godsey, ed., Preface to Bonhoeffer, Philadelphia: Fortress Press, 1965, p. 32). In this instance, however, Bonhoeffer is encouraging the Christian to love the earth on account of its belonging to God and His Kingdom. He is not arguing here, and does not argue until after 1939, that the Christian should ever love the earth for its own sake, with a relative independence of God or Christ. It is this relative independence from Christ and His purposes which Bonhoeffer urges explicitly in the Letters which is the subject of our inquiry.

[2] In Sanctorum Communio, Bonhoeffer disagrees with Karl Barth on the manner in which the Christian is to love his neighbor. Barth had argued in The Epistle to the Romans that the believer is to love God in the other, a position which Bonhoeffer rejected in favor of a more direct love. He insisted that the Christian was to love the person in himself, for in appreciating the Thou which is his neighbor, the believer experiences God's claim upon himself. For our purposes, it should be pointed out that neither Barth nor Bonhoeffer approved here a purely secular love, or eros, for the neighbor in relative independence from Christ. Both understandings of love of neighbor were based upon the mediation of Jesus Christ and, though differently construed, are in contrast to the view proposed by Bonhoeffer after 1939.

[3] See earlier references to earthly desires cited in Chapter I. See especially The Cost of Discipleship, pp. 106, 107, 196, and 109, 110.

[4] Dietrich Bonhoeffer, Letters and Papers from Prison (enlarged edition, New York: Macmillan Paperback, 1972), p. 303.

[5] This dating follows the sequence proposed by Eberhard Bethge in his preface to the sixth German edition of the Ethics. The International Bonhoeffer Society, in as yet unpublished papers, has

essentially substantiated Bethge's arrangement.

[6]Later, in Chapter IV, Bonhoeffer explicitly argues that the "good" in life is not thoroughly godless but, rather, is put into place by God Himself as a measure to preserve earthly life. The Christian needs to distinguish this worldly good and evil in order to make important decisions. This notion of the good and the value of knowing it are fundamental to his treatment of "The Natural".

[7]Dietrich Bonhoeffer, Ethics (New York: Macmillan Publishing Co., 1976), p. 18.

[8]Ibid., p. 19.

[9]Ibid., p. 21.

[10]Letters and Papers from Prison, pp. 176, 177.

[11]Ethics, p. 20.

[12]Ibid., pp. 25, 26.

[13]Ibid., p. 27.

[14]Ibid., p. 32. Bonhoeffer emphasizes that judgment is evil because of its essential relationship to man's disunion: "...judgment is evil because it is itself apostasy, and that is also the reason why it brings forth evil fruit in the human heart. It cannot, of course, be denied that from the psychological point of view extremely noble motives may also be disclosed as determining the thought of the man who judges, but this fact can have no bearing on the character of the judging itself. 'Judging' is not a special vice or wickedness of the disunited man; it is his essence, manifesting itself in his speech, his action, and his sentiment". Having condemned the actions of the Pharisee in an absolute sense, Bonhoeffer will alter, elaborate upon, and endorse the "extemely noble motives" and the "impartial and earnest" judgment of the Pharisee as somehow genuinely "good" in themselves.

[15]Ibid., p. 31.

[16]Ibid., p. 19.

[17]Ibid., p. 31.

[18]Ibid., p. 34, 35.

[19]Ibid., p. 35.  As Bonhoeffer puts it, "The new knowledge of the reconciliation which is accomplished in Jesus, the knowledge of the voiding of the disunion, itself entirely voids man's own knowledge of his own goodness...  A man's own goodness is now concealed from him... The situation is quite clear:  knowing of Jesus a man can no longer know of his own goodness, and knowing of his own goodness he can no longer know of Jesus (pp. 34, 35)".

[20]Ibid., pp. 31, 46

[21]Ibid., p. 48.

[22]Ibid., p. 50.  Yet, there is a form of love which persists in the midst of disunited life, a love which is recognized by all persons: "Everything that we are accustomed to call love, that which lives in the depths of the soul and in the visible deed, and even the brotherly service of one's neighbour which proceeds from a pious heart, all this can be without 'love', not because there is always a 'residue' of selfishness in all human conduct, entirely overshadowing love, but because love as a whole is something entirely different from what the word designates here".  The "love" which remains in fallen life is not the love of Christ, hence it is not love at all, and yet it may arise from a "pious" heart, and is acknowledged as love by persons nevertheless.

[23]Ibid., pp. 50, 51.

[24]Ibid., p. 53.

[25]Bonhoeffer makes a similar distinction between Christian and natural love in The Cost of Discipleship: "What is undivided love?  Love which shows no special favour to those who love us in return.  When we love those who love us, our brethren, our nation, our friends, yes, and even our own congregation, we are no better than the heathen and the publicans.  Such love is ordinary and natural, and not distinctively Christian.  We can love our kith and kin, our fellow-countrymen and our friends, whether we are Christians or not, and there is no need for Jesus to teach us that".  The Christian love, he continues, is distinctive in that it can love with the love of Christ.  This makes the believer's love "extraordinary", for he can love even his enemy.  It is this Christ-like love which sets the Christian apart so that he "cannot live at the world's level..."  Later, Bonhoeffer will specifically urge and encourage this "natural love"

upon the Christian for its own sake. See The Cost of Discipleship, pages 169-171 for the above distinction.

[26]Letters, pp. 41, 42.

[27]Ethics, p. 53.

[28]Letters and Papers from Prison, p. 42.

[29]Ethics., pp. 53, 54.

[30]Ibid., pp. 55, 59.

[31]Ibid., p. 60.

[32]Ibid., p. 61.

[33]Bonhoeffer's experience in the resistance movement surely contributed to this broader theory on the human values to which persons commit themselves and the worth of their devotion to human causes. The simple characterization of such persons as hypocrites, engaging in "self-deception" and "false-doing" was inadequate in describing the complex experienced reality of the resistance and his fellow-collaborators as he had come to know them. He needed to give a fuller account of the positive pole of the Christian dialectic interpreting earthly life.

[34]Ibid., p. 62. It remains true that the "good" people stand before Christ as sinners, but yet they are good, unlike the wicked, and in their willingness to suffer on behalf of the values retained in earthly life they somehow "find their way back to Christ...(61)". Bonhoeffer claims that his analysis of human good is not an exercise in the abstract, but describes his own experience. While he does not say so, it seems safe to assume that Bonhoeffer speaks of persons he had come to know in the resistance movement whose devotion to the cause had issued in their discovery of common ground with Christians and, ultimately, with Christ.

[35]The relationship of Christ to these people is an intimate one. In contrast to Christians who are paralyzed by their desire to "act rightly" (p. 60), "good" people are willing to devote themselves to just, good and true causes, and to suffer on their behalf. Although the causes to which they devote themselves do not entail the confession of His name, Christ is said to protect such people, claim them, take responsibility for them, and draw them toward Himself.

[36]Ibid., pp. 61, 62.

[37]Ibid., p. 61.

[38]Ibid., p.38.

[39]Ibid., p. 57.

[40]Ibid., p. 57.

[41]Ibid., p. 58.

[42]Ibid., p. 58.

[43]Ibid., p. 58.

[44]Ibid., p. 58.

[45]Dietrich Bonhoeffer, The Cost of Discipleship (New York: Macmillan Paperback, 1968), pp.313, 314. In these pages, Bonhoeffer accentuates the separation of the Church from the world. He writes: "The community of saints is barred off from the world by an unbreakable seal, awaiting its ultimate deliverance. Like a sealed train travelling through foreign territory, the Church goes on its way through the world... The sanctification of the Church means its separation from all that is unholy, from sin... All this has a threefold significance for the community of saints. First, their sanctification will be maintained by their being clearly separated from the world. Secondly, it will be maintained through their walking in a way which is worthy of the holiness of God. Thirdly, their sanctification will be hidden, and they must wait for the day of Jesus Christ... For the Spirit seals off the Church from the world". While this is a particularly negative appraisal of the earth, it does not necessarily represent a contradiction in Bonhoeffer's thought. It may simply be a harsh statement of the negative pole of the dialectic, a powerful reminder that, in its fallenness, the earth is without value before God and offers nothing of worth to the Christian. It is worthy of note, however, that Bonhoeffer does not focus upon this pole of the dialectic in the Letters and Papers from Prison. A major shift in what he affirms, develops and explains takes place in the later writings.

[46]According to Eberhard Bethge, this chapter of the Ethics was written by Bonhoeffer in September of 1940. See the Editor's Preface to the Sixth German edition of the Ethics, p. 12.

[47]These lectures were later reproduced as <u>Christ</u> <u>the</u> <u>Center</u>, ed. by Eberhard Bethge, trans. by John Bowden (New York: Harper and Row, 1966). In these lectures, Bonhoeffer explains how Christ ontologically structures reality in Himself. His argument that Christ becomes the center of man's existence, history and nature is qualified: "The character of the statement about his centrality is not psychological, but ontological-theological" (62).

[48]<u>Ethics</u>, p. 71.

[49]<u>Ibid</u>., p. 89.

[50]<u>Ibid</u>., pp. 74, 77.

[51]Bonhoeffer describes this life as follows: "To be formed in the likeness of the Crucified - this means being a man sentenced by God. In his daily existence man carries with him God's sentence of death, the necessity of dying before God for the sake of sin. With his life he testifies that nothing can stand before God save only under God's sentence and grace. Every day man dies the death of a sinner... To be conformed with the Risen One - that is to be a new man before God. In the midst of death he is in life. In the midst of sin he is righteous. In the midst of the old he is new... The new man lives in the world like any other man. Often there is little to distinguish him from the rest (<u>Ethics</u>, pp. 81, 82)".

[52]<u>Ibid</u>., p. 79.

[53]<u>Ibid</u>., p. 79.

[54]<u>Ibid</u>., p. 71.

[55]<u>Ibid</u>., p. 79.

[56]<u>Ibid</u>., p. 89. Bonhoeffer expresses this tension as follows: "The 'yes' and the 'no' which God addresses in history in the incarnation and crucifixion of Jesus Christ introduces into every historical instant an infinite and unresolvable tension. History does not become a transient vehicle, but through the life and death of Jesus Christ it does for the first time become truly temporal. It is precisely in its temporality that it is history with God's consent. Consequently, when we ask about the historical inheritance we are not asking the timeless question about those values of the past of which the validity is eternal. Man himself is set in history and it is

for that reason that he now asks himself about the present and about the way in which the present is taken up by God in Christ." This description of the dialectical tension inherent in earthly life was presented in Bonhoeffer's Barcelona writings in 1929 (see note 67 below), but now, in the winter of 1940-1941, he writes affirmatively for the first time of the fallen, earthly pole of that dialectic.

[57] Ibid., p. 120.

[58] Ibid., p. 120.

[59] Ibid., p. 120. Bonhoeffer will continue to insist upon the absolute freedom of God in the gracious activity of revelation. In a tone reminiscent of Luther and Barth, he resists any theology from below, and will not permit any human transcendence which moves unaided towards the divine. Man's redemption can come only from above and, until the arrival of the word of grace into human life, it remains irretrievably lost and judged. Nevertheless, human life has been entered by the "force" of God's reconciliation, since life is preserved and encompassed in the event of Christ. For this reason, life must be understood in the many shades of dark and light which His presence creates.

[60] Ibid., p. 122. Bonhoeffer describes man's separation from God in this way: "He never knew [before prior to his justification in Christ] what life is. He did not understand himself. Only by his own potentialities or by his own achievement could he try to understand himself and to justify his life... he could have no means of access to the potentialities and the works of the living God; he could have no conception of a life which should proceed from these potentialities and the works of the living God. He could not conceive of a life on a foundation other than himself, sustained by a power other than his own." Yet it is significant that it is this same reliance upon one's achievements and potentialities which will constitute the "natural" pole in the dialectic of earthly life which Bonhoeffer affirms later in Chapter IV.

[61] Ibid., p. 123. This word proceeds solely from God. Man cannot earn it, produce it, or assist in its coming: "...it is therefore never the natural or necessary end of the way which has been pursued so far, but it is rather the total condemnation and invalidation of this way. It is God's own free word, which is subject to no compulsion... Consequently, it excludes any method of achieving it by a way of one's own."

[62]Ibid., p. 133.

[63]Ibid., p. 125.

[64]Ibid., p. 125.

[65]This is a dilemma which Bonhoeffer did not take seriously prior to 1939. In an address to his congregation in Barcelona on January 25, 1929 entitled "What is a Christian Ethic?", Bonhoeffer spoke of the contradiction which the believer faced as he confronts earthly life. But Bonhoeffer does not affirm the fallen, natural pole of the dialectic here, and does not do so until after 1939. In 1929, he spoke as follows: "But through this freedom from the law, from principle, the Christian must enter into the complexity of the world; he cannot make up his mind a priori, but only when he himself has become involved in the emergency and knows himself called by God. He remains earthbound, even when his desire is towards God; he must go through all the anxiety before the laws of the world; he must learn the paradox that the world offers us a choice, not between good and evil, but between one evil and another, and that nevertheles God leads him to himself even through evil." It is important to note that after 1939, Bonhoeffer explicitly affirms the relative good of natural life, and encourages the believer to desire those earthly goods for their own sake. These affirmations are absent from the Barcelona address. See No Rusty Swords (New York: Harper and Row, 1965), pp. 39-48.

[66]Ethics, p. 125.

[67]The Cost of Discipleship, pp. 106, 107.

[68]Ethics, p. 127.

[69]Once again, we note Bonhoeffer finding fault with a position which was essentially his own before 1939. The documentation we have presented from earlier works shows Bonhoeffer separating the penultimate from the ultimate in a far more unqualified fashion than he does now.

[70]Ethics, p. 127.

[71]Ibid., p. 127.

[72]Ibid., p. 127.

[73]Ibid., p. 130.

[74]Ibid., p. 129.

[75]Ibid., pp. 130, 131.

[76]Ibid., p. 132.

[77]Ibid., p. 131.

[78]Ibid., p. 133.

[79]Ibid., p. 142.

[80]Ibid., pp. 133, 134.

[81] Ibid., p. 139. Bonhoeffer denies that the improvement of the penultimate will usher in the arrival of grace, or that its neglect can prevent the success of the Word. It is "Christ alone" Who "creates faith (p. 141)." Still, the hearing of the Word can be facilitated or rendered more difficult depending upon the relative quality of human life. The Christian is called to recognize this fact, and to enhance the penultimate as the realm to which the Word of grace is to be addressed.

[82]Ibid., p. 139.

[83]Ibid., p. 139.

[84]Ibid., p. 140.

[85]Ibid., pp. 141, 142.

[86]See Note 10.

[87]In what follows, reference will be made to Chapter I and II of the Ethics, "The Love of God and the Decay of the World", and "The Church and the World". The contrast between these earlier sections of the Ethics, written, as Bethge has told us, before the fall of 1940, and the materials presently under consideration (written in the winter of 1940-1941) illuminates the crucial turn in Bonhoeffer's thinking which is the focal point of our inquiry.

[88]Ibid., pp. 142, 143.

89Ibid., p. 46. As we will suggest, the actions of the rich young ruler, understood in the light of his unbelief, can be similarly described. But Bonhoeffer will add to this description a consideration of his relative goodness for which Jesus loves him.

90Ibid., p. 35. "The situation is quite clear: knowing of Jesus a man can no longer know of his own goodness, and knowing of his own goodness he can no longer know of Jesus. Man cannot live simultaneously in reconciliation and in disunion, in freedom and under the law, in simplicity and in discordancy. There are no transitions or intermediate stages here; it is one thing or the other." Yet, later, in urging the believer to know the natural by his reason, he insists that the Christian know his own goodness and perform it.

91Ibid., p. 27. In purely human terms, the Pharisee is entirely respectable. To regard him as less than exemplary on this level is to miss the import of Jesus' criticism. "The Pharisee," says Bonhoeffer, "is that extremely admirable man who subordinates his entire life to his knowledge of good and evil and is as severe a judge of himself as of his neighbour to the honour of God, whom he humbly thanks for this knowledge."

92Ibid., p. 27.

93Ibid., pp. 26, 27.

94Ibid., p. 38. As we have seen, the Pharisee, at his best, represents man at his worst in relation to God. In his obsession with the judging and performing of the "right", the Pharisee reveals his passion for his own disunion: "...judgment is evil because it is itself apostasy, and that is also the reason why it brings forth evil fruit in the heart. It cannot, of course, be denied that from the psychological point of view extremely noble motives may also be disclosed as determining the thought of the man who judges, but this fact can have no bearing on the character of judgment itself" (p. 32). The Pharisee, then, is wrong in judging the good on his own, but Bonhoeffer does not yet deal with the question of whether in fact some of his judgments may be true or relatively valuable. His reference to the "extremely noble motives" of the Pharisee may be an anticipation of Bonhoeffer's later affirmation of "goodness" in fallen life, but, as we have argued earlier, it is only implied here.

95Ibid., p. 143.

[96]Ibid., p. 143.

[97]Ibid., p. 145.

[98]Ibid., p. 145.

[99]Ibid., p. 145.

[100]Ibid., p. 144, 145. Bonhoeffer stresses the significance of natural life even for those to whom Christ has already come. The natural is not, then, merely a sphere in which unbelievers enjoy a relative freedom with respect to God; the faithful are also to participate in, and enjoy, the relative freedom of the natural life. This is a distinct advance over Chapters I-III of the Ethics and also a massively significant one by which Bonhoeffer turns to a whole new area of inquiry, namely, the positive significance for the believer of the fallen world as fallen. This is a major turning point in the book.

[101]Ibid., p. 163.

[102]Ibid., p. 149.

[103]ibid., p. 145.

[104]Ibid., p. 145.

[105]Ibid., pp. 145, 146.

[106]Ibid., p. 146.

[107]Ibid., p. 147.

[108]Ibid., p. 147.

[109]Ibid., p. 147.

[110]Ibid., p. 148.

[111]Ibid., p. 148.

[112]Ibid., p. 149.

[113]Ibid., p. 149.

[114]Ibid., p. 149.

[115]Ibid., p. 150.

[116]Ibid., p. 150.

[117]Ibid., p. 150.

[118]Ibid., p. 151.

[119]Ibid., p. 151.

[120]Ibid., p. 151.

[121]See Creation and Fall, pp. 73ff.  Here Bonhoeffer describes the results of the Fall on earthly life without the subtlety of his discussion of The Natural.  He writes: "The defection is continual falling, a plunging into bottomless depths, a being relinquished, a withdrawal ever farther and deeper.  And in all this it is not simply a moral lapse but the destruction of creation by the creature.  The Fall affects the whole of the created world which is henceforth plundered of its creatureliness as it crashes blindly into infinite space, like a meteor which has torn away from its nucleus (p. 77)."

[122]Ethics, pp. 156, 154.

[123]Ibid., p. 156.

[124]Ibid., p. 158.

[125]Ibid., p. 158.

[126]Ibid., p. 156.

[127]Ibid., p. 151.

[128]Ibid., p. 154.

[129]Ibid., p. 151.

[130]Ibid., p. 147.

[131]Ibid., p. 148.

132Ibid., p. 155.

133Ibid., p. 155.

134Ibid., p. 149.

135Letters, pp. 191, 192, 176, 177.

136Ethics, p. 145.

137Ibid., p. 203.

138Ibid., p. 188. Bonhoeffer describes this dialectic as follows: "So far we have been speaking of the world only in the sense of the world which is reconciled with God in Christ. We have spoken of reality always in the sense of the reality which is taken up, maintained and reconciled in God. And it is in this sense that we have had to reject all thinking that is conducted in terms of two spheres. But this still leaves open the question whether the 'world', if by this we understand the 'disordered' world which has fallen under the power of the devil, and whether sinful reality ought perhaps to be conceived as a space or realm which is established in oppo- sition to the Church or to the kingdom of Christ" (p.203). The answer to this question is found in the ultimate reconciliatory achievement in Christ in which the world remains "disordered" in its fallenness, but still relatively "good" in its independence from Christ.

139Ibid., p. 195.

140Ibid., p. 197.

141Ibid., p. 198.

142Ibid., p. 188.

143Ibid., p. 188.

144Ibid., p. 197. Bonhoeffer discusses the origin and development of this misleading conception of earthly life as follows: "Since the beginning of Christian ethics after the times of the New Testament the main underlying conception in ethical thought, and the one which consciously or unconsciously has determined its whole course, has been the conception of a juxtaposition and conflict of two spheres, the one divine, holy, supernatural and Christian, and the other worldly, profane, natural and un-Christian... In all these schemes the cause of Christ becomes a partial and provincial matter within the limits of reality. It is assumed that there are realities which lie outside the reality that is in Christ... However great the importance which is attached to the reality of Christ, it still always remains a partial reality amid other realities. The division of the total reality into a sacred and a profane sphere, a Christian and a secular sphere, creates the possibility of existence in a single one of these spheres, a spiritual existence which has no part in secular existence, and a secular existence which can claim autonomy for itself and can exercise this right of autonomy in its dealings with the spiritual sphere..." (196, 197). Bonhoeffer's stress upon the novelty of his theses indicates his conviction that he was saying something new. He invoked Scripture and Martin Luther because he believed the tradition had lost the original insights of these sources.

[145]Ibid., p. 197.

[146]Ibid., p. 198.

[147]Ibid., p. 200.

[148]Ibid., p. 198.

[149]Ibid., p. 139.

[150]Ibid., p. 199. For support of notion of the polemical inter-dependence of the secular and the Christian, Bonhoeffer appeals to Luther and his doctrine of the two kingdoms. He argues that Luther protested with the help of the secular against a Christianity which was "striving for independence and detaching itself from the reality in Christ." With Luther, Bonhoeffer claims that the polemical relationship of the secular and the Christian produces a better form of each. "It is only in this sense," Bonhoeffer writes, "as a polemical unity, that Luther's doctrine of the two kingdoms is to be accepted, and it was no doubt in this sense that it was originally intended." This notion of polemical unity is a significant advance of the Ethics development because, as we argue, the fact that the secular has a right to fight and assert itself against the Christian is a new approach to the affirmation of the goodness of the fallen world. Anticipating his critics, Bonhoeffer claims that his concept is not new to Lutheran theology, but is traceable to Luther himself. But Bonhoeffer was also aware that the interpretive hand which he placed upon Luther was discontinuous with the tradition of Lutheran orthodoxy.

[151]Ibid., pp. 191, 192, 193.

[152]Ibid., p. 203.

[153]Ibid., p. 205.

[154]Ibid., p. 204.

[155]Ibid., p. 204.

[156]Ibid., p. 206.

[157]Ibid., p. 205.

[158]Ibid., p. 207.

[159]Ibid., p. 207.

[160]The mandates of government and the Church do not function in the same manner because they are different in character. Government is structured to serve a preservative role: "Government cannot itself produce life or values. It is not creative. It preserves what has been created, maintaining it in the order which is assigned to it through the task which has been imposed by God." (210) The Church, on the other hand, is qualitatively different from the other three mandates: "This mandate is the task of enabling the reality of Jesus Christ to become real in the preaching and organization of the Church and the Christian life. It is concerned, therefore, with the eternal salvation of the whole world. The mandate of the Church extends to all mankind, and it does so within all the other mandates (211)."

[161]Ibid., p. 209.

[162]Ibid., p. 209.

[163]Ibid., p. 210.

[164]Ibid., p. 211.

[165]Ibid., pp. 217, 218, 221.

[166]Ibid., p. 215. Bonhoeffer explains his aversion to such ethi-

cal systems as follows: "Ethical thought is still largely dominated by the abstract notion of an isolated individual man who applies the absolute criterion of a good which is good in itself and has to make his decision incessantly and exclusively between this clearly recognized good and an equally clearly recognized evil. Already, with what we have said previously, we have left this notion behind us. These isolated individuals do not exist and we do not dispose over any such absolute criterion of a good which is good in itself; nor do good and evil display themselves in history in their pure form (214, 215)."

[167]Ibid., pp. 215, 216.

[168]Ibid., p. 218.

[169]Ibid., pp. 219, 220.

[170]Ibid., pp. 218, 219.

[171]Ibid., p. 89.

[172]Ibid., pp. 219-220.

[173]Ibid., p. 220.

[174]Ibid., p. 220.

[175]Ibid., pp. 255, 256.

[176]Ibid., p. 222.

[177]Ibid., p. 225.

[178]Ibid., p. 224.

[179]Ibid., p. 226.

[180]Ibid., pp. 235, 236.

[181]Ibid., p. 236.

[182]This chapter, according to Bethge, was written in the winter of 1942-1943, only months before his imprisonment, but some six months after the completion of Chapter VI. See Bethge's Preface

to the sixth German edition of the <u>Ethics</u>, p. 13.

[183]<u>Ethics</u>, p. 265.

[184]<u>Ibid</u>., p. 267.

[185]<u>Ibid</u>., pp. 267, 268.

[186]<u>Ibid</u>., pp. 268, 269.

[187]<u>Ibid</u>., p. 280.  As Bonhoeffer explains on page 268, life's ultimate ethical obligation "goes without saying", and is thereby rendered virtually inoperative for daily life by its own self-evident character.  It is so obvious, in effect, that it is not necessary to make a topic of discussion.  This fact, in turn, releases persons to partake freely in life's flow, through "unreflected doing."

[188]<u>Ibid</u>., p. 299.

[189]<u>Ibid</u>., p. 147.

[190]<u>Ibid</u>., p. 266.

[191]As we indicated earlier, the ethical only becomes a theme for discussion when the self-evident way of life is endangered, when life in the family, marriage or one's labor is jeopardized.  At that point, the ethical speaks firmly to restore what is under attack.  As Bonhoeffer explains:  "'Shall' and 'should' make themselves heard only at the point where this fellowship is disrupted or the organization is endangered, and as soon as order is restored, they have nothing more to say. (266)."

[192]<u>Ibid</u>., p. 269.

[193]<u>Ibid</u>., p. 269.

[194]<u>Ibid</u>., p. 277.

[195]<u>Ibid</u>., p. 280.  Bonhoeffer describes the role of the commandment of God at some length: "God's commandment, revealed in Jesus Christ, embraces the whole of life.  It does not only, like the ethical, keep watch on the untransgressible frontier of life, but it is at the same time the centre and fullness of life.  It is not only obligation but also permission.  It does not only forbid, but it also sets free for life; it sets free for unreflected doing."  By this repeated reference to

"unreflected doing", Bonhoeffer stresses that the Christian is often not conscious of God as he lives fully in the natural life.

[196]Ibid., pp. 298, 299.

[197]Ibid., p. 299.

[198]Ibid., pp. 280-284.

[199]Ibid., p. 283.

[200]Ibid., p. 283.

[201]Ibid., p. 282.

[202]Ibid., p. 282.

[203]Ibid., p. 298.

# CHAPTER IV
## BONHOEFFER ON EARTHLY DESIRES:
## DOES HE SOLVE THE PROBLEM?

To conclude, we return to where we began and ask the question which prompted our inquiry, namely, why does Bonhoeffer encourage and urge Christians in the Letters and Papers from Prison to long for their absent loved ones and other good things of the earth for their own sake?  The question focuses upon a theme which is conspicuous by its absence in Bonhoeffer's work before 1939.  Until that time, purely secular yearnings are described as "dark desires", and sharply contrasted with genuine brotherly love, or agape, created in the Christian heart by the Holy Spirit.[1]  Human, or purely secular desires are acknowledged, tolerated, and even declared to be of some use, but they are never praised, encouraged or urged for themselves.  The extolling and encouraging of earthly desires, therefore, particularly the longing of loved ones to be with one another, is new to the Bonhoeffer corpus and suggests deeper shifts in his theological anthropology and ethics.  The purpose of our study is to present Bonhoeffer's answer to the question stated above in the Letters, and to indicate further reasons for the encouragement of secular desires in the Ethics, a fragmented work for which Bonhoeffer produced the first drafts after his return to Germany and before his arrest in 1943.  In this final chapter we will summarize our findings: a) how Bonhoeffer extols secular desires in the Letters and what grounds he gives for this evaluation, and b) certain ways in which the Ethics clarifies this encouragement.  Next, we will compare and contrast the discussion of earthly desires in the two works, and assess the coherence of Bonhoeffer's call to a life without God before God as it manifests itself in the believer's secular longing for absent loved ones for their own sake in relative abstraction from the person of Christ.  Then, with reference to Larry Rasmussen's criticism of Bonhoeffer's ethical methodology, we will conclude with questions and suggestions for further discussion and inquiry.

We did not argue to developments in Bonhoeffer's theology from concurrent experiences in his personal life.  But there are "turning-points" in Bonhoeffer's life to which scholars assent with virtual unanimity,[2] and Bonhoeffer himself stated repeatedly how much his personal experience influenced his thinking.  In the light of Bonhoeffer's own statements and the evident parallels between his thought and life, our Chapter II provides a confirmatory historical context for the theological developments for which we later argued.

The experience of deprivation and yearning which aborted Bonhoeffer's 1939 visit to New York returned with crushing force after his imprisonment in 1943.  The accompanying pain was particularly difficult for Bonhoeffer to bear because, as he admitted in a letter to Bethge, he "lived for many, many years quite absorbed in aims and tasks and hopes without any personal longings."[3] Confessing that he had often taken life's good things and other persons "for granted",[4] Bonhoeffer now discovered that "nothing tortures us more than longings."[5] Before his final years, certainly prior to 1939, Bonhoeffer had not been forced to live without the good things of life and had lived, in large part, without passion. Now with the course of his life so drastically altered, and moved by his yearning for the success of the resistance movement, his affection and respect for his co-conspirators, his love for Maria, and his emptiness in the absence of his closest friend, his theology began to accommodate the experience of intense, secular longings which had become so large a part of his life.

As he faced the prospect of death, Bonhoeffer grappled with the meaning of his own life, and with the value of the constellation of risks, responsibilities and loves which he had woven into it. Tormented by "accidie, tristitia, with all its menacing consequences",[6] Bonhoeffer wondered if his yearnings, which he acknowledged as secular in nature, were worth the suffering they generated. One cannot read the Letters without sensing the pain and self-doubt which Bonhoeffer experienced.

Many Christians of his time, as Bonhoeffer himself noted, responded to the converging pressures of separation and deprivation by belittling the purely earthly desires which generated them. These Christians, following a more traditional course, tried to give as little time, attention and energy to human feelings as possible and devote themselves instead to their faith in Christ and the perspectives it yielded. Bonhoeffer, however, chose to encourage his desiring, to urge himself and others to feel their longings fully and thereby live rich, multi-dimensional lives. He also chose to see God as not merely permitting this devotion to earthly life, but as urging this kind of involvement upon the Christian as an appropriate expression of faith. Bonhoeffer sought this encouragement for two distinct, yet related reasons. First, he needed encouragement because he wanted to continue to feel his love for others as a part of his own polyphonous life. Encouragement was required because the loneliness of prison life was often unbearable, and the suppression of desires offered the path of least resistance. In addition, Bonhoeffer wanted encouragement because his political decisions had also issued in enormous suffering and anxiety. Ironically, his devotion to earthly life had served to deny him the very life he loved. He needed to be assured that his fundamental choice on behalf of earthly life and its values had been justified, and that God supported him in the resulting deprivation. There was a side of Bonhoeffer which wanted to stop desiring and end the suffering which his multiple longings engendered. He needed assurance that God somehow urges the kind of involvement with others and with earthly life which epitomized Bonhoeffer's last years, and which generated his secular yearnings. Mere permission or toleration of such longing, present in the Lutheran tradition, did not strengthen him sufficiently to face his desires and to bear the full weight of the pain. In the Letters, then, we see Bonhoeffer build upon the Ethics and provide an account of Christian faith which lends theological support to the believer's purely secular desires.

Bonhoeffer advanced several propositions on human longing in the Letters which do not appear in his work before 1939. They give some answers to our central question, while still needing clarification. Our question was, "Why does Bonhoeffer encourage and urge Christians in the Letters to long for their absent loved ones and the other good things of the earth for their own sake?" In Chapter I, we culled from the Letters these elements of an answer:

1) It is good or valuable to feel personal, secular longings for loved ones.

2) The longing is experiential riches.

3) We thank God for it, because, like earthly joy, it is a part of our love for God's precious gift of human life.

4) To feel such longings fully is an achievement which requires arduous concentration and toil.

5) This achievement consists in full, sustained concentration on the absent one or the thing desired, and on the feeling of longing itself.

6) This willed concentration yields a mastery of the desire, which brings inner order,wholeness, freedom, and energy to live the rest of one's life fully.

7) Love for Christ (cantus firmus) helps to develop this passionate, secular longing to its full independence and wholeness.

144

8) Our nature urges us to feel our longing, for only thus can we be united with our loved one, even in separation.

This survey raised several questions. Why is it good or valuable to feel secular longings for loved ones? What does Bonhoeffer mean by the notion of "good" in "good" things of the earth, when understood in relative independence from God? Why does God want our erotic, earthly longings to develop as powerfully as possible, to their full independence and wholeness? Why is it important for Christians to feel a full, complete passion for their loved ones? How does the cantus firmus assist in the achieving of mastered desires? In what sense is the desire of the Christian for a loved one a distinct entity wholly for itself? In what sense is it independent of Christ and yet related to Him? Finally, how does the mastering of purely secular yearnings make us more fully human?

Our study of the Ethics was intended to throw light upon these matters and to suggest an explanation for Bonhoeffer's related call to a "life without God before God." In our study we, in fact, discovered that the Ethics is a dynamic advance over the writings prior to 1939 which progresses steadily into the secular theology of the Letters. As our analysis in Chapter III has indicated, there are several significant assertions in the Ethics which clarify Bonhoeffer's encouragement of secular desires in the Letters and his call to Christian life "as if there were no God". These correlative assertions are listed below:

1) The Christian is urged to live the Natural life (Chapter IV)
 a) This life is fallen, and enjoys a relative freedom from Christ and His purposes.
 b) This life is endowed with rights which are the gifts of God to fallen, natural life. These rights are the "reflected splendour of the glory of God's creation."
 c) These rights to bodily life and bodily joys are to be enjoyed as "ends in themselves" for all persons.
 d) Human joy in these rights is spoiled by any thought of purpose.
2) This fallen life is able to create its own values (Chapter V)
 a) Through the mandates of labor and marriage, persons enter into the "will of the Creator" and share in the "process of

creation."

    b) Fallen secular life has the right to ad-
monish and correct the Church when it fails
to foster earthly values.

3) God speaks a "yes" and "no" to fallen life
(Chapters III & VI)

    a) Fallen life, in general, contradicts our
life in Christ.

    b) Yet the Christian is to participate in
earthly life insofar as it opposes Christ
only by failing to experience or recognize
His presence.

4) The only warrant for ethical discourse is
the commandment of God (Chapter VII)

    a) The commandment of God permits the
process of life to flow uninterruptedly.

    b) The commandment of God allows
Christians to live freely, unburdened
by the ethical.

    c) The commandment of God removes moral
anxiety and brings certainty, trust, peace,
confidence, inner continuity and unity to
living.

    d) The commandment of God commands
freedom to live structured, natural life.

    As we place these propositions alongside those gleaned from
the Letters, we see a disparity in terminology, but a striking conver-
gence of meaning. Beginning in Chapter IV of the Ethics and continuing throughout the prison writings Bonhoeffer encourages
Christians to participate in fallen, earthly life as vigorously as the
non-Christian, and to do so in relative independence from Jesus
Christ. The believer is to live fully in the world which does not know
Christ, seeking and enjoying its good things for their own sake. In
living the fallen, natural life, the believer assists life in reaching its
intended form, and also discovers the polyphonous way of life which
enhances his own humanity. He can only live this life with the
assistance of his love of God (cantus firmus), for without it, he cannot
hear the all-embracing "yes" and "no" addressed to earthly life in
Christ, nor keep in proper perspective the relationship of the
ultimate and the penultimate. God wants our erotic yearnings to
develop as completely as possible because in desiring life and its good
things we become one with the "underlying will" of preserved life
and with the will of God Who gives that life as His gift. Only in
affirming the "yes" to natural life can we, at the same time, hear the
"no" of God which judges and condemns that life. It is out of the

146

unceasing tension of the "yes" and the "no" that the Christian is called to live. The fallen life of the Christian is independent of Christ and rejects Him only by failing to recognize His presence; yet it is structured in Him through the mandates and natural rights to be lived "as if there were no God." The pursuit of earthly joys and values is an end in itself for all persons in relative independence from Christ, and yet it is also a means to an end in enriching human experience and in carrying out God's will for the penultimate.

What, precisely, therefore, has Bonhoeffer done? From Chapter IV in the Ethics until his death, Bonhoeffer consistently affirmed and developed a view of Christian life which is found nowhere else in his work. In essence, the Christian is called to live in Christ, in an absolute sense, and without Him, independent of Him, insofar as he lives his daily natural life. God Himself commands this freedom and encourages the believer to enjoy it, and to find therein the fullness and abundance of life.

This commandment may still be described as an ethic of conformation (Ethics, Chapter III) insofar as it urges the believer to seek out the reality of God in the reality of the world reconciled in Christ, but there are significant changes in the account. The structure of the ethical life founded upon the commandment of Jesus Christ is radically unlike the guide to moral action proposed as late as Chapter III in the Ethics. There Bonhoeffer spoke of ethics as "conformation to Christ" (Gleichgestältung) and action "in accordance with reality" (Wirklichkeitsgemässheit).[7] The basis for this conceptualization is the ontological taking-form of Christ in reality as proposed in Christ the Center, carried on through the early Ethics, and then revised, subtly but profoundly, from Chapter IV on the natural and throughout his writing thereafter. In the Christology lectures, Bonhoeffer understood reality as thoroughly Christological in character, and directly so. Thus, he asserts that Christ's centrality amidst human existence, history and nature is to be understood ontologically: "The character of the statement about his centrality", he argues, "is not psychological but ontological-theological."[8] In partaking in the reality of the world, one was said to be drawn directly into the form of Jesus Christ. When Bonhoeffer says "not psychologically", he leaves room for the relative independence and value of natural life from the person of Christ, and thereby affirms a different dimension of "conformation" and Christian living.

From Chapter IV onwards, Bonhoeffer argues that Christ encourages the Christian to carry out His will precisely by living the natural, godless life. The believer conforms to Christ by living as if

He were not present, in relative independence from Him and His purposes. In short, we wish to argue that in Chapter IV, Bonhoeffer begins to affirm a dimension of the Christian's life in a different way than he did before 1939, and that he affirms this life with increasing clarity culminating in his call in the Letters for life "without God before God", as manifested in purely secular desires for absent loved ones.

Eberhard Bethge, in his Preface to the sixth German edition of the Ethics, claims that Bonhoeffer's work in the Ethics contains four distinct theological starting-points.[9] The third, which he labels "justification", is said to be played out in Chapters IV and V in the present arrangement of the Ethics. The fourth starting-point, "incarnation", characterizes the present chapters VI and VII. We wish to argue that Bethge's fourth starting-point is actually a continuation of the third which was determinative for Bonhoeffer and which served as a foundation for his Christian ethic until his death. Our inquiry shows that Chapter IV marks a decisive theological turning point after which all that Bonhoeffer writes serves to develop and clarify the themes he introduced there.

As we saw in our Chapter III, Bonhoeffer makes claims in Chapters VI and VII based upon the nature of Christ's incarnation which advance his account of earthly life considerably. We refer here especially to his extended treatment of the "yes" and "no" addressed to fallen reality, the duty of the secular to assert its rights and values vîs-a-vîs the Church, the ability of fallen life to create values, and the commandment of God which sets believers free in Jesus Christ to live human life to its fullest. But these assertions are not discontinuous with the structure and direction of Chapter IV. There he claimed that the penultimate, while an "empty jest" with respect to the ultimate, was to be "taken seriously in its own way", and that it had been endowed with natural rights, including the right to bodily joys. These rights, he argued, were the "reflected splendour of the glory of God's creation", and were to be enjoyed as ends in themselves by all persons. The assertions of Chapters V-VII explore and unpack this conception of fallen life introduced in Chapter IV. Bonhoeffer's line of thought, though drawn with increasing subtlety, is essentially continuous from Chapter IV until his death. His fourth "starting-point" and provocative remarks in the Letters are attempts to respond to his own experience and to add greater depth to the Christ-centered depiction of earthly life established in his discussion of the natural.

A major result of his encouragement to the natural life is that the ethical becomes peripheral. The believer is simply urged to live, and the life formed in the mandates is almost without exception self-evident. As we saw in Chapter VII of the Ethics, Bonhoeffer explicitly asserts that ethics, as traditionally conceived, has only a tangential relation to Christian life. In fact, when the ethical is firmly entrenched on the boundaries of life where it properly belongs, natural life flows freely as intended, as in the case of personal longings. When one freely desires, and acquiesces to the natural life, the ethical is a spectator to the human drama.[10] It is not consulted, and in the absence of divisive moral conflicts, the ethical becomes a silent partner to the flow of life. What we have, therefore, is an ethic almost entirely without ethics, or living without wrenching decision-making in the normal course of the moral life.[11] The question of what one "ought" to do rarely arises because the natural life is meant to be lived unreflectedly.[12] In the free acceptance of the structure of natural life, one leaves ethical conflicts behind. This is a major departure from moral philosophy in general and, as Bonhoeffer realizes, a momentous advance in the understanding of Christian ethics.

Larry Rasmussen's thoughtful criticism of Bonhoeffer's ethic is very helpful in elucidating this shift in his thought.[13] Rasmussen accuses Bonhoeffer of failing to establish a basis for assessing different claims to Christian action, all of which assert that they bring about God's will.[14] Rasmussen argues, with substantial reliance upon Chapters I-III of the Ethics, that Bonhoeffer cannot help the believer with the hard questions of Christian ethics because he does not provide any measurements by which to advocate one action over another.[15] He finally arrives at two conclusions which are significant for our inquiry. The first is a judgment of Bonhoeffer's ethical methodology; the second is his final evaluation of that method's success. With respect to the method itself, Rasmussen writes as follows:

> In the end Bonhoeffer's ethic is essentially a Gesinnungsethik and suffers the shortcomings thereof. Such a claim would strike objection from Bonhoeffer himself, and so a careful explication of terms is necessary, as well as the claim. A Gesinnungsethik denotes an ethic of disposition; it claims that what really matters for ethics happens in the formation of the moral agent. An Objektivethik denotes an ethic of norms or patterns of moral behavior which exist independent of the agent. This ethic focuses on acts, means, and goals, whereas a Gesinnungsethik by contrast

directs its attention to the condition of the moral subject. The propensity of an <u>Objektivethik</u> is to provide clear and definable public criteria for evaluating and testing action, whereas the propensity of a <u>Geninnungsethik</u> is to provide the measurements for character formation... The claim is that Bonhoeffer's is a <u>Gesinnungsethik</u> because what counts is the formation of the self into Christ's form, formation occurring in communion with the living Christ; furthermore, and decisively, the testing of Christian action is referred to the self's preparation for receiving Christ's concrete command. What really matters for ethics happens in character formation.[16]

His conclusion, which follows careful argumentation, is that Bonhoeffer's ethic is ultimately unsatisfying:

The question posed was whether Bonhoeffer's methodology and understanding of ethics are adequate. The conclusion is that they are not because they work against answering the test question of Christian ethics: how am I, as a Christian, to decide among conflicting claims, all of which contend that they embody the will of God?[17]

The present author believes Rasmussen to be mistaken on both counts insofar as he has misrepresented Bonhoeffer's program from Chapter IV in the <u>Ethics</u> onward. In reading the later portions of the <u>Ethics</u> as developments internal to the structure of Chapters I-III, Rasmussen fails to recognize the major shift which occurs in Chapter IV and which alters the character of Bonhoeffer's ethic from there on. Bonhoeffer's ethic, as it evolves after 1940 is neither a <u>Gesinnungsethik</u> nor an <u>Objektivethik</u> in the true sense. It is not the former because the ethic is decidely personalistc and relational, consistently concerned with action, non-action, and their effect upon human life. As we stressed throughout the study, Bonhoeffer is passionately devoted to earthly life for its own sake, and rejects pious motivations to action which draw believers away from that life. The godliest of intentions and deliberations, insofar as they issue in a withdrawal from natural life, are denied validity. It is terribly important to Bonhoeffer that persons be properly motivated in weighing the course of their moral action, and that they seek the course which appears most life-enhancing. But it is equally important to

Bonhoeffer that they <u>do</u> that which actually accords with reality as structured by Christ. Christian deliberation which results in action contrary to earthly life is of dubious value at best. This is why Bonhoeffer questions the faith of the believer who withdraws from earthly life in refusing to desire its good things: "To renounce a full life and its real joys in order to avoid pain is neither Christian nor human."[18] Devotion to earthly life issues from appropriate Christian decision-making and vice versa.

Bonhoeffer's ethic is also not an <u>Objektivethik</u>, but not for the reasons Rasmussen suggests. The commandment of God to the Christian to live natural life does focus upon the actions with which one responds to that command. One is called to live, and to do so fully. Further, norms and patterns of moral behavior, of a kind, do exist imbedded in the structure of formed, earthly life. One violates life insofar as one promotes the destruction of the mandates and their interrelationship, or insofar as one violates the rights accorded natural life. These mandates and rights serve as norms, structures and rules to which all rational beings have access and to which all are held accountable. With these elements in place, Bonhoeffer cannot and does not advocate a radical contextual ethic; the context of decision-making is always filled in large measure by the mandates and natural rights. But, despite this inherent structure, Bonhoeffer's ethic is not adequately described as <u>Objektivethik</u> for the "norms" which fill life are not of the usual variety. They are not abstract principles to which one must regularly appeal in order to justify action; rather, they are constituent elements of life which are to be desired and enjoyed naturally, and, for the most part, unreflectedly, without conscious reference to their relative validity. As the believer lives daily in "unreflected doing", he does not tirelessly seek out the appropriate norms to guide to his every action. Instead, he simply desires the structure of life and lives it. The mandates and rights of natural life are not intended to resolve perpetual ethical conflicts, but to transcend them. Through the structure of fallen reality, daily living becomes essentially "pre-ethical."[19] The mandates and rights of natural life provide a structure in which living is self-evident, and free, for the most part, of ethical deliberation. As a result, Bonhoeffer argues, natural life flows smoothly and persons experience a certitude, confidence, clear direction and firm security in their daily lives, released by the commandment of God to enjoy the unfolding process of life.

Bonhoeffer's ethic establishes a life bordered by the ethical but lived without it, except in exceptional circumstances. It is not without any structure, for if it were, the Christian would face each moment without direction of any sort and lack the confidence which

Bonhoeffer insists he enjoys. On the contrary, life is so thoroughly formed by self-evidently desirable mandates and rights that decision-making becomes a natural part of the "all-embracing unity" of one's life.

Rasmussen's conclusion that Bonhoeffer's ethics are finally inadequate is based upon the false assumption that the question Rasmussen brings to the text is the one Bonhoeffer is asking after 1940. Rasmussen's test question of Christian ethics, namely, "how am I, as a Christian to decide among conflicting claims, all of which contend that they embody the will of God?", is exactly the question Bonhoeffer wished to leave behind. In Chapter VII of the Ethics, Bonhoeffer makes it clear that Rasmussen's question places ethics in the midst of life's flow where it wrongly impedes and interrupts life by raising moral conflicts where none exist. The commandment of God is not meant to serve as a final arbiter of ethical dilemmas, but as the basis upon which such conflicts come to an end. Bonhoeffer does not want to adjudicate absolute competing moral claims; he wants to relativize them. In urging believers to become part of the flow of natural life, free from the fear of constant moral choice, Bonhoeffer believed that the commandment of God succeeded in removing this conflict from the daily process of life.

Bonhoeffer has attempted to shift the discussion of ethics from the realm of day-to-day life to the exceptional situation, in which the flow of natural life is threatened. Only when the structure of fallen life is endangered does the ethical play a role. At this level, Bonhoeffer succeeds, and this is a profound achievement. The vast majority of decisions are not to be mulled over at great length; one simply desires life's inherent structure as it wills the individual and life itself toward its intended fulfillment. One merely acts that life and oneself be enriched. The precise action one chooses is not critical. What is critical, however, is that one seek to live fully, in accord with reality, and trust that choices made in that freedom are life-affirming. Confidence, certainty, quietude and peace are said to result.

But extreme circumstances do arise, and with them come moral problems:

> There are, of course, undoubtedly occasions
> and situations in which the moral course is
> not self-evident, either because it is not, in
> fact, followed or because it has become ques-
> tionable from the point of view of its con-
> tents. It is at such times that the ethical

becomes a theme... These occasions, when the
ethical becomes a theme for discussion, pur-
ify and restore the human community and are
necessary for it, and yet, precisely because
of the essential character of this theme, they
must always be considered only as exceptional occurrences.[20]

However, even in the midst of these exceptional situations, Bonhoeffer's call to live structured life fully enables him to find a
measure of peace in the midst of ethical conflict. Rasmussen claims
that Bonhoeffer's ethic cannot handle the extreme cases of ethical
decision-making, and argues from the example of tyrannicide that
Bonhoeffer's own sense of guilt demonstrates its failure:

Yet in practical decision-making Bonhoeffer
shows ambivalence and perhaps methodo-
logical irresolution here. As we have noted he
experienced a great deal of guilt in executing
'the deed of free responsibility', in carrying
out 'the exceptional command'. Ostensibly
the reason is that the law, especially divine
law, remains a strong penultimate norm for
Bonhoeffer, and its violation thus incurs guilt.
The appropriate question for method is: what
is the relation of the radical contextualism
to the penultimate norms, to the generalized
configuration of Christ's form in a 'filled'
contextual ethic? If one stands by an ethic
of 'the concrete command' of 'concrete
instruction in the concrete situation', as
Bonhoeffer claims a true Christian ethic is,
it is difficult to see why a commanded
'violation' of the penultimate norms should
incur guilt for him who is obedient.[21]

Once again, Rasmussen appears to have missed the essential
shift in Bonhoeffer's approach to ethics. In choosing to live structured life fully under the commandment of God, Bonhoeffer is not
torn by moral choice but confidently carries out actions self-evidently
in accord with reality. The case of tyrannicide does not pose an
extreme ethical dilemma for Bonhoeffer because he does not confront
the problem in the manner Rasmussen suggests. Instead, he con-
sults the basic guidance of the mandates and the rights of natural
life as he does in his discussions of euthanasia and abortion in

Chapter IV.[22]   There he establishes the fundamental principles of protection of innocent life, non-interference with the natural order of the world, and the rule that one enjoys the rights of natural life only so long as one respects the rights of others.  Acting within this structure of formed life, one must simply do what is required to protect, preserve and enhance natural life.  In short, one is set free to live.  Bethge's recollection of Bonhoeffer's response to the hypothetical case of a runaway driver is very apt here:  "He (Bonhoeffer) stated that, as a pastor, it was his duty, not only to comfort the victims of the man who drove in a busy street like a maniac, but also to try to stop him."[23]

In the case of Hitler, Bonhoeffer followed a similar course.  It was self-evident that Hitler's tyrannical rule was in gross violation of the mandates and the rights of natural life;  no extensive ethical reflection was required to make that determination.  It was equally clear that, for the sake of life itself, Hitler must be stopped in the most effective manner possible.  Joining the plot to remove Hitler and, at the same time, preventing his replacement by another tyrant was not a decision over which Bonhoeffer brooded at great length.  It flowed naturally from his desire for life itself, without respect to the ethical as such.

Rasmussen's claim that Bonhoeffer experienced guilt over his decision to take part in the plot rests upon his interpretation of Bonhoeffer's poem, "Prison".  There Bonhoeffer speaks of guilt because he knows that through his choice he will incur guilt in the eyes of others.  His arrest and imprisonment are proof of Bonhoeffer's point, as was the subsequent unwillingness of many Christians to honor Bonhoeffer for his sacrifice.  From the point of view of the ethical, Bonhoeffer was judged guilty by many and rejected by those who could not approve of his moral choice.  But in his own eyes, Bonhoeffer had merely acted judiciously and intelligently in order that the cause of life itself be fully served.  Transcending the ethical, Bonhoeffer felt little, if any, guilt himself.  As the poem suggests, he stood confident before his accusers,[24] and sought forgiveness only for failing to act more quickly and for being a part of a fallen world in which wretched choices must often be made.  In the case of tyrannicide, Bonhoeffer's devotion to natural life and not his devotion to ethics was the source of his decision and his courage.

This is not to say that Bonhoeffer did not have second thoughts about his decisions.  It is clear that he experienced considerable suffering as a result of his participation in the resistance.  But he does not engage in the sort of ethical self-scrutiny and re-assessment suggested by Rasmussen. Instead, he ponders the larger issue of his decision to live natural life fully, the choice from which his actions smoothly and self-evidently followed. He is not questioning his ethical judgment, but his fundamental commitment to earthly life for which he suffers so greatly.

Bonhoeffer's decision to commit himself to natural life generated two untraditional ways of living. First, where other Christians repressed their human longings or dismissed them as base urges, Bonhoeffer rejoiced in them and claimed that they drew him more deeply into the flow of life. His intense personal longings were a natural outgrowth of his decision to live earthly life to the fullest. Secondly, he refused to take part in the perpetual conflict of the ethical. He was willing to acknowledge competing ethical claims, but relativized them so that any choice made in accord with the structure of formed life was legitimate. Even in extreme cases, such as tyrannicide, his course of action was self-evident. One simply seeks to affirm life where it is threatened and takes the action required to restore life to its natural flow. Removing Hitler was no more excruciating a moral choice than a decision to remove the "maniac" driving so as to endanger others.

For our purposes, however, Bonhoeffer's basis for decision-making is not of interest primarily at the level of ethical theory, but because it is closely related to his work on earthly desires. As we earlier suggested, Bonhoeffer often wanted encouragement to continue to bear the pain which resulted from his commitment to others and to earthly causes, particularly the resistance movement. He occasionally had ambivalent feelings about the decisions he had made with respect to natural life, and needed assurance that he had acted rightly. His work on secular desires brought him some measure of assurance, enough to lend strength and counsel to Bethge on occasion. But a troubling "accidie" tormented him nevertheless. The point is that Bonhoeffer at times lacked certainty and confidence in the choice he had made. Living earthly life fully, and feeling one's personal longings to the utmost was an extremely arduous task. At times, he felt himself living polyphonous life vibrantly and powerfully, and during those moments he wrote encouragingly to Bethge of the _cantus firmus_ and the mastering of desires. But at other times he was haunted by doubts and suffered horribly. Insecurity, self-doubt, depression and even thoughts of suicide weighed upon him. His poignant and repetitious references in Chapter VI of the _Ethics_ to the certitude, confidence, trust and security afforded by the commandment of God to live natural life freely appear to be attempts to convince himself as well as his readers. His theology of human longing helped give him some of the

155

assurance and encouragement which he sometimes needed to live fully.

In addition to his replacement of ethics with the freedom of the commandment of God, as exemplified in his account of personal longings, Bonhoeffer has implicitly offered a revised conception of the Christian self. He alters traditional notions of sanctification, arguing that one becomes "holy" in fully living fallen, natural life. The Ethics, thereby, makes clear what Bonhoeffer meant when he spoke of "holy worldliness" in the Letters. Abundant life in Christ consists in devotion to fallen reality under His "yes" and "no", in obedience to God Who encourages this multi-dimensional life and makes it possible. Becoming a "new creation" in Christ no longer draws one out of earthly life but more deeply into it, as exemplified in God's urging of human longings. Instead of seeking union with God on a higher, spiritual plane, the Christian is called to discover God in the center of life, paradoxically finding Christ as he appears to lose Him, in fallen secular reality. It is the very nature of the believer to live in this manner, and all of life, the Christian himself, and even the purposes of God are fulfilled in the living of natural life. The further one strays from the earth, the further one moves away from God, and the more one lives independently of God, "without God", the more completely one finds Him.

In essence, we see now what Bonhoeffer intended in his enigmatic letter to Bethge in May of 1944. The cantus firmus, or the Christian's love of God, grants and encourages an independence to the contrapuntal themes of earthly life. One never abandons the cantus firmus, for without it multi-dimensional life is impossible. Yet one can, in a relative sense, develop secular themes such as earthly love to their complete wholeness, in one sense reliant upon the cantus firmus, and still independent from it. In the Ethics, this rich perspective on earthly life is foreshadowed in the "yes" and "no" addressed by God to fallen reality. Only in hearing the "no" can the believer fully appreciate the "yes" of affirmation to earthly life, and only when the "yes" is enjoyed to the fullest as an end in itself must it be called back the "no" to the reality of life under God. Like the cantus firmus, God's "yes" and "no" permits life a relative independence and yet binds it to its Source.

As Bonhoeffer brooded over the cantus firmus and the call to Christians to live fallen life to the fullest, he became more deeply assured that he had acted rightly:

> During the last year or so I've come to know
> and understand more and more the profound

> this-worldliness of Christianity. The
> Christian is not a <u>homo</u> <u>religiosus,</u> but simply
> a man, as Jesus was a man - in contrast, shall
> we say, to John the Baptist. I don't mean the
> shallow and banal this-worldliness of the
> enlightened, the busy, the comfortable, or the
> lascivious, but the profound this-worldliness,
> characterized by discipline and the constant
> knowledge of death and resurrection ...I'm
> still discovering right up this moment,
> that it is only by living completely in this
> world that one learns to have faith.[25]

Bonhoeffer's account of secular desires, and his willingness after 1939 to affirm the earthly pole of the dialectic of fallen life, has led us to deeper, more fundamental shifts in his theology. Bonhoeffer's ethics, as we have seen, is unique to Christian thought. No other Christian thinker, to my knowledge, has encouraged and urged believers to live natural life for its own sake as vigorously as the non-Christian. Nor has anyone argued that God Himself urges earthly joys and this relative independence upon the Christian as an expression of his faith and as essential to multi-dimensional, polyphonous human life. One only becomes fully Christian and fully human when one lives "without God before God". The <u>Letters</u>, then, are not radically discontinuous with all of Bonhoeffer's prior work; they proceed, in fact, directly from Chapter IV of the <u>Ethics</u>. But both the <u>Ethics</u> and the <u>Letters</u> affirm, encourage, and develop at much length, a conception of Christian life and of earthly desires which is nowhere to be found in Bonhoeffer's work before 1939, and perhaps nowhere else in Christian theology. But can the Christian genuinely be at peace in the natural life, as Bonhoeffer suggests? Is the believing self able to live wholeheartedly in a life which knows nothing of his Lord? What is the precise nature of the "good" which the Christian experiences in godless life when only God is good? Is there an "implicit" Christianity in those unbelievers who sacrifice themselves for earthly life, and live a form of "holy worldliness" without reference to Christ? As we saw, these are questions which Bonhoeffer has not answered completely and unambiguously. But his account of purely human desires is bold and insightful in its characterization of daily Christian life and the role of the ethical.

Perhaps if Bonhoeffer had lived longer, he might have experienced the inner peace given in the commandment of God more consistently, and offered a more detailed account of the Christian's secular life and of the relationship of the <u>cantus</u> <u>firmus</u> to the living of multi-dimensional natural life. It may be that the dignity and composure which he brought to his execution were signs of a deeper personal confidence which may later have found more complete theological expression. But it is enough that Bonhoeffer accomplished as much as he did. His unique call to Christians to revere the life reconciled in Christ and to live that life "without God" and yet "before God" is a challenge understood by few and accepted by fewer. If this study has served to cast Bonhoeffer's challenge before Christians once again and to advance, in some small measure, an appreciation of its power and radicality, then this work will have succeeded to my satisfaction.

## Notes to Chapter IV

[1] We have documented this negative appraisal of secular desires at some length in Chapter I of this study.

[2] No scholar, to my knowledge, has rejected Bethge's well-documented and argued notion of turning-points in Bonhoeffer's life and thought. Debate continues over the precise dating of the first turning-point, but there appears to be no debate about the turning-points themselves. I use the expression "virtual unanimity", therefore, in the event that there is dissent on this matter of which I am unaware.

[3] Dietrich Bonhoeffer, Letters and Papers from Prison (enlarged edition, New York: Macmillan Paperback, 1972), p. 271.

[4] Ibid., p. 305.

[5] Ibid., p. 167.

[6] Ibid., p. 129.

[7] Dietrich Bonhoeffer, Ethics (New York: Macmillan Publishing Co., 1976), p. 80.

[8] Dietrich Bonhoeffer, Christ the Center (New York: Harper and Row, 1966), p. 62.

[9] Ethics, pp. 11-14.

[10] Ibid., p. 266.

[11] Ibid., pp. 264, 265.

[12] Ibid., pp. 280, 283.

[13] Larry Rasmussen, Dietrich Bonhoeffer: Reality and Resistance (New York: Abingdon Press, 1972). See Part III, "Critique of Methodology", pp. 149-173.

[14] Ibid., p. 151.

[15] I indicate Rasmussen's reliance upon Chapters I-III because I wish to argue that he has not fully grasped the shift in Bonhoeffer's ethic which begins in Chapter IV. As a result, he criticizes Bonhoeffer for holding a position which he abandons, in

large measure, after Chapter III.

[16]_Ibid._, p. 158.

[17]_Ibid._, p. 168.

[18]_Letters_, p. 191.

[19]_Ethics_, p. 283.

[20]_Ibid._, p. 267.

[21]_Rasmussen_, p. 152.

[22]_Ethics_, pp. 160ff.

[23]Eberhard Bethge, _Dietrich Bonhoeffer: Man of Vision, Man of Courage_ (New York: Harper and Row, 1970), p. 755.

[24]Bonhoeffer writes:
> But now, with both freedom and honour de-
> nied, before men we can hold up our heads in
> pride, And if we are brought into evil fame,
> we ourselves before men can clear our name.
> Man against man, our ground we choose,
> and we the accused will in turn accuse.

See Dietrich Bonhoeffer, "Prison", _Union Seminary Quarterly Review_, March, 1946, pp. 6-8.

[25]_Ethics_, p. 267.

# Bibliography

## A) Primary Sources

Sanctorum Communio. Eine dogmatische Untersuchung zur der Kirche, 1930; 3rd Edition, Munich: Chr. Kaiser, 1960.

Akt und Sein. Transcendentalphilosophie und Ontologie in der systematischen Theologie, 1931; Munich: Chr. Kaiser, 1956.

Schopfung und Fall. Theologische Auslegung von Genesis 1 bis 3, 1934; Munich: Chr. Kaiser, 1958.

Nachfolge, 1937; 9th Edition, Munich: Chr. Kaiser, 1967.

Gemeinsames Leben, 1939; 12th Edition, Munich: Chr. Kaiser, 1966.

Ethik, ed. by Eberhard Bethge, 1949; 7th Edition, Munich: Chr. Kaiser, 1966.

Widerstand und Ergebung (Neuausgabe), ed. by Eberhard Bethge; Munich: Chr. Kaiser, 1970.

Gesammelte Schriften, ed. by Eberhard Bethge; Vols. 1-4, Munich: Chr. Kaiser, 1958-1961, Vols. 5-6, Munich: Chr. Kaiser, 1972-1974.

Fragmente Aus , ed. by Renate and Eberhard Bethge; Munich, Chr. Kaiser, 1978.


## In Translation

The Communion of Saints. Trans. by Ronald Gregor Smith et. al., New York, Harper & Row, 1963.

Act and Being. Trans. by Bernard Noble, New York: Harper & Row, 1962.

"Concerning the Christian Idea of God." The Journal of Religion. XII.2 (April, 1932), 177-185.

"Thy Kingdom Come. The Prayer of the Church for God's Kingdom on Earth." Trans. by John Godsey, Preface to Bonhoeffer, 28-47.

Creation and Fall: A Theological Interpretation of Genesis 1-3. Trans. by John Fletcher et. al. New York: Macmillan, 1959.

The Cost of Discipleship. Trans. by R.H. Fuller. New York: Macmillan, 1963.

Temptation. Trans. by Kathleen Downham. New York: Macmillan, 1955.

Life Together. Trans. by John W. Doberstein. New York: Harper & Row, 1954.

Psalms: The Prayer Book of the Bible. Trans. by James H. Burtness. Minneapolis: Augsburg, 1970.

Ethics. Trans. by Neville Horton Smith. New York: Macmillan, 1955.

Letters and Papers from Prison. Trans. incorporates the text of the third English edition produced by Reginald Fuller, Frank Clarke and others; additional material by John Bowden. New York: Macmillan Paperbacks, 1972.

No Rusty Swords. Letters, Lectures and Notes, 1928-1936, from the Collected Works of Dietrich Bonhoeffer, Vol. I. Trans. by Edwin H. Robertson and John Bowden. New York: Harper & Row, 1965.

The Way to Freedom. Letters, Lectures and Notes, 1935-1939, from the Collected Works of Dietrich Bonhoeffer, Vol. II. Trans. by Edwin H. Robertson and John Bowden. New York: Harper & Row, 1966.

True Patriotism. Letters, Lectures and Notes, 1939-1945, from the Collected Works of Dietrich Bonhoeffer, Vol. III. Trans. by Edwin H. Robertson and John Bowden. New York: Harper & Row, 1973.

Christ the Center. Trans. by John Bowden. New York: Harper & Row, 1966.

I Loved This People. Testimonies of Responsibility. Trans. by Keith R. Crim. Richmond, Virginia: John Knox Press, 1965.

"The Other Letters from Prison." Trans. by Maria von Wedermeyer in her article in the Union Seminary Quarterly Review. XXIII.1 (Fall, 1967), 23-29.

Fiction from Prison: Gathering Up the Past. Translated by Ursula Hoffmann. Philadelphia: Fortress, 1981.

B) Secondary Sources

Altizer, Thomas J.J. and William Hamilton. Radical Theology and the Death of God. New York: Bobbs Merrill, 1966.

Andrews, Allan R. "Bonhoeffer's Psychology: Humanistic Ally or Christian Corrective?" Christian Scholar's Review 4.1 (1974), 16-25.

Armstrong, C.B. "Christianity Without Religion." New Theology No. 2, 17-27. Edited by Martin E. Marty and Dean C. Peerman. New York: Macmillan, 1965.

Arnould, E.R. "Who's Afraid of Dietrich Bonhoeffer? A Comparison of Bonhoeffer and Albee." Journal of Religious Thought 29:1 (1972), 57-75.

Ballard, Paul H. "Camus and Bonhoeffer: Living in a Godless World." Theology LXXVIII. 662 (August,1975), 418-428.

Bartley, W.W. "The Bonhoeffer Revival." The New York Review of Books V.2 (August 26, 1965), 14-17.

Bebis, George S. "Bonhoeffer and the Fathers of the Church" a reply to Brightman." Lutheran Quarterly XXIV.3 (August, 1972), 273-279.

Berger, Peter L. "Camus, Bonhoeffer and the World Come of Age." The Christian Century LXXVI (April 8 & 15, 1959), 417-418.

Bethge, Eberhard. "Bonhoeffer's Christology and His 'Religionless Christianity.'" Union Seminary Quarterly Review XXIII.1 (Fall, 1967), 61-77.

_____. Bonhoeffer: Exile and Martyr. Edited and with an Essay by John W. de Gruchy. London: Collins, 1975.

_____. "The Challenge of Dietrich Bonhoeffer's Life and Theology." The Chicago Theological Seminary Register LI.2 (February, 1961), 1-38.

_____. Dietrich Bonhoeffer: Man of Vision, Man of Courage. New York: Harper & Row, 1970.

_____. "Editor's Foreword" to Bonhoeffer, Letters and Papers from Prison, third edition, revised and enlarged, London and New York, 1967.

_____. "Editor's Preface to the Newly Arranged Sixth German Edition" [of Bonhoeffer's Ethics]. Preface to the rearranged edition, London and New York, 1963ff., but lacking in pre-1969 printings of this edition.

_____. "Turning Points in Bonhoeffer's Life and Thought." Union Seminary Quarterly Review XXIII.1 (1967), 3-21.

Bosanquet, Mary. The Life and Death of Dietrich Bonhoeffer. Foreword by Sabine Leibholz-Bonhoeffer. New York: Harper & Row, 1969.

Bowden, John S. and James Richmond, eds. A Reader in Contemporary Theology. Philadelphia: Westminster, 1967. Introduction by the editors (103-104) to a selection from Bonhoeffer's Letters and Papers from Prison under "Dietrich Bonhoeffer: The Non-Religious Interpretation of Biblical Concepts."

Bowman, Douglas C. Bonhoeffer's Methodology for Describing the Nature of Man Under Grace in the Modern Context. Ph.D. dissertation, unpublished: San Francisco Theological Seminary, 1963.

Conner, William F. "The Laws of Life" A Bonhoeffer Theme With Variations." Andover Newton Quarterly 18.2 (Nov., 1977), 101-110.

Coughlin, K. "The Concept of World in the Thought of Dietrich Bonhoeffer." Insight 7 (Summer, 1969), 18-22.

Cox, Harvey. "Beyond Bonhoeffer: The Future of Religionless Christianity." Commonweal XLIII.21 (September 17, 1965), 653-657.

Day, Thomas I. "Communal Sense, Anyone?" New Catholic World 215.1286 (September-October, 1972), 225ff.

_____. "Conviviality and Common Sense: The Meaning of Christian Community for Dietrich Bonhoeffer." A Bonhoeffer Legacy: Essays in Understanding, 213-236. Edited by A.J. Klassen. Grand Rapids, Michigan: Wm. B. Eerdmans Publishing co., 1981.

De Jong, Pieter. "Camus and Bonhoeffer on the Fall." Canadian Journal of Theology VII.4 (October, 1961), 245-257.

Downing, F. Gerald. "Man's Coming of Age: Dietrich Bonhoeffer and Christianity Without Religion." Prism VI.8 (December, 1962),

31-42.

Dumas, Andre. Dietrich Bonhoeffer. Theologian of Reality. Translated by Robert McAfee Brown. New York: Macmillan, 1971.

Feil, Ernest. The Theology of Dietrich Bonhoeffer. Translated by Martin Rumscheidt. Philadephia: Fortress, 1985.

Fennell, William O. "The Theology of True Secularity." New Theology No. 2, 28-38. Edited by Martin E. Marty and Dean G. Peerman. New York: Macmillan, 1965.

Foley, Grover. "Christianity, Religion and Humanism." Austin Seminary Bulletin LXXX.1 (September, 1964), 3-20.

Godsey, John D. Preface to Bonhoeffer: The Man and Two of His Shorter Writings. Philadelphia: Fortress, 1965.

_____. "Reading Bonhoeffer in English translation: Some Difficulies." Union Seminary Quarterly Review XXIII.1 (Fall, 1967), 79-90.

_____. "Theologian, Christian, Contemporary." [Review article on Bethge, Dietrich Bonhoeffer.] Interpretation XXV.2 (April, 1971), 208-211.

_____. The Theology of Dietrich Bonhoeffer. Philadelphia: Westminster, 1960.

_____. "Bonhoeffer's Understanding of Love." Unpublished paper read at meeting of the International Bonhoeffer Society, at Dallas, Texas in 1980.

Green, Clifford James. "Bonhoeffer's Concept of Religion." Union Seminary Quarterly Review XIX.1 (November, 1963), 11-21.

_____. "Interpreting Bonhoeffer: Reality of Phraseology?" [Review article on Ott, Reality and Faith, and Dumas, Dietrich Bonhoeffer. Theologian of Reality.] Journal of Religion 55.2 (April, 1975), 270-275.

_____. "Sociality and Church in Bonhoeffer's 1933 Christology." Scottish Journal of Theology 21.4 (December, 1968), 416-434.

_____. "Bonhoeffer in the Context of Erickson's Luther Study."

Psychohistory and Religion. The Case of 'Young Man Luther', 162-196. Edited by Roger A. Johnson. Philadelphia: Fortress, 1977.

_____. The Sociality of Christ and Humanity: Dietrich Bonhoeffer's Early Theology, 1927-1933. Missoula, Montana: Scholars Press, 1975.

Griffin, Graeme Maxwell. The Self and Jesus Christ: a critical consideration of the nature of the self and its place in Christian theology and life, with particular reference to the thought of Dietrich Bonhoeffer and Carl G. Jung. Th.D. dissertation, unpublished: Princeton Theological Seminary, 1965.

Hamilton, William. "A Secular Theology for a World Come of Age." Theology Today XVIII.4 (January, 1962), 435-459.

Hopper, David. H. A Dissent on Bonhoeffer. Philadelphia: Westminster, 1975.

Jenkins, Daniel. Beyond Religion. The Truth and Error in "Religionless Christianity." Philadelphia: Westminster, 1962.

Jenkins, David E. "Bonhoeffer and the Mistake of Looking to Data about God." Guide to the Debate about God, 90-106. Edited by David E. Jenkins. Philadelphia: Westminster, 1966.

Johnson, Roger A. "Dietrich Bonhoefer: Religionless Christianity - Maurity, Transcendence and Freedom." Roger A. Johnson, Ernest Wallwork, et al., Critical Issues in Modern Religion. Englewood Cliffs, New Jersey: Prentice-Hall, 1973.

Jung, Carl G. "Religionless Christianity." Journal of the American Academy of Religion XXXIX.1 (March, 1971), 43-47.

Kelly, Geffrey B. "An Interview with Jean Lasserre." Union Seminary Quarterly Review XXVII.3 (Spring, 1972), 149-160.

_____. "Bonhoeffer's 'Non-religious' Christianity: Antecedents and Critique." Bisdragen 37 (1976), 118-148.

Kelley, James Patrick. "Bonhoeffer Studies in English: How theologians became popular." Lexington Theological Quarterly III.1 (January, 1968), 12-19.

_____. "Bonhoeffer's Legacy: 'After Its Bloom.'" Journal of Religious Thought 39:1 (Spring, Summer, 1982), 46-52.

166

_____. Revelation and the Secular in the Theology of Dietrich Bonhoeffer. Ann Arbor, Michigan: University Microfilms International, 1981.

Kemp, Walter H. "The 'Polyphony of Life': References to Music in Bonhoeffer's Letters and Papers from Prison." Vita Laudanda: Essays In Memory of Ulrich S. Leupold, 137-154. Edited by Erich R.W. Schultz. Waterloo, Ontario, Canada: Wilfrid Laurier University Press, 1976.

Klassen, A.J., ed. A Bonhoeffer Legacy: Essays in Understanding. Grand Rapids, Michigan: Wm. B. Eerdmans Publishing Co., 1981.

Kuske, Martin. The Old Testament as the Book of Christ: An Appraisal of Bonhoeffer's Interpretation. Translated by S.T. Kimbrough. Philadelphia: Westminster, 1976.

Lehmann, Paul L. "Bonhoeffer: Real and Counterfeit." [Review article on The Communion of Saints and No Rusty Swords.] Union Seminary Quarterly Review XXI.3 (March, 1966), 364-369.

_____. "Faith and Worldliness in Bonhoeffer's Thought." Union Seminary Quarterly Review XXIII.1 (Fall, 1967), 31-44.

Leibholz-Bonhoeffer, Sabine. The Bonhoeffers: Portrait of a Family. Foreword by Lord Longford. Preface by Eberhard Bethge. New York: St. Martin's Press, 1971.

Lillie, W. "Worldliness of Christianity." Expository Times LXXV (February, 1964), 132-137.

Lindbeck, George. "Demythologizing of Dietrich Bonhoeffer." Commonweal 96 (September 29, 1972), 527-528.

McLaren, D.M. A Study in the theology of Dietrich Bonhoeffer, with particular reference to Christian spirituality. M. Th. thesis, unpublished. Glasgow University, 1976.

Macquarrie, John. "Religionless Christianity." God and Secularity, Chapter V. Philadelphia: Westminster, 1967.

Mark, J. "Bonhoeffer from Prison, I: Man's Coming of Age." Prism VI.1 (January, 1962), 67-72.

_____. "Bonhoeffer from Prison, II: Christianity Without

Religion." Prism VI.2 (February, 1962), 57-64.

Marty, Martin E. "Bonhoeffer: Seminarians Theologian." The Christian Century LXXVII (April 20, 1960), 467-469.

_____, ed. The Place of Bonhoeffer. Problems and Possibilities in His Thought. New York: Association Press, 1962.

Milhaven, John Giles. "How far has God shared his dominion with man?" American Ecclesiastical Review (January, 1970), 57-63.

_____. "The Enjoyment of Earthly Goods for Its Own Sake." Unpublished paper read to the International Bonhoeffer Society meeting in New York, November, 1979.

_____. "Dietrich Bonhoeffer on Earthly Desire." Unpublished paper read to the International Bonhoeffer Society meeting in Oxford, England, March, 1980.

Moltmann, Jurgen. "The Lordship of Christ and Human Society." In Moltmann and Weissbach, Two Studies in the Theology of Bonhoeffer. New York: Charles Scribner's Sons, 1967.

Moltmann, Jurgen and Jurgen Weissbach. Two Studies in the Theology of Bonhoeffer. Translated by Reginald and Ilse Fuller. Introduction by R.H. Fuller. New York: Charles Scribner's Sons, 1967.

Morris, Leon. The Abolition of Religion. A Study in "Religionless Christianity." Chicago: Intervarsity Press, 1964.

Mosely, N. "Religionless Christianity." Prism VI.6 (October, 1962), 1-3.

Mottu, Henry. "Feuerbach and Bonhoeffer: Criticism of Religion and the Last Period of Bonhoeffer's Thought." Translated from the French by David Lewis. Union Seminary Quarterly Review XXVI.1 (Fall, 1969), 1-18.

Niebuhr, Reinhold. "Dietrich Bonhoeffer." Union Seminary Quarterly Review I.3 (1946), 3.

Oden, Thomas C. Contemporary Theology and Psychotherapy: Chapter II: "Bonhoeffer's Theology and Religionless Psychotherapy." Philadelphia: Westminster, 1967.

Ott, Heinrich. "The Difference: What Practical Difference Does it Make if We Believe in God?" Translated by John Winslow. <u>Drew Gateway</u> 40.3 (Spring, 1970), 122-134.

_____. Reality and Faith: <u>The Theological Legacy of Dietrich Bonhoeffer</u>. Philadelphia: Fortress, 1972.

Peck, William. "A Proposal Concerning Bonhoeffer's Concept of the Person." <u>Anglican Theological Review</u> L.4 (October, 1968), 311-329.

Phillips, John A. <u>Christ for Us in the Theology of Dietrich Bonhoeffer</u>. New York: Harper, 1967.

Rasmussen, Larry L. <u>Dietrich Bonhoeffer: Reality and Resistance</u>. Nashville: Abingdon Press, 1972.

Reynolds, Terrence. "Dietrich Bonhoeffer's Encouragement of Human Love: A Radical Shift in His Later Theology." <u>Union Seminary Quarterly Review</u> 41:3,4 (1987), 55-76.

Robinson, John A.T. <u>Honest to God</u>. Philadelphia: Westminster, 1963.

Robinson, John A.T. and David L. Edwards. <u>The Honest to God Debate</u>. Philadelphia: Westminster, 1963.

Ruether, Rosemary. "A Query to Daniel Sullivan: Bonhoeffer on Sexuality." <u>Continuum</u> 4.3 (Autumn, 1966), 457-460.

Schmidt, Karl. <u>Rediscovering the Natural in Protestant Theology</u>. Minneapolis, Minnesota: Augsburg Press, 1962.

Schneider, Edward S. "Bonhoeffer and a Secular Theology." <u>Lutheran Quarterly</u> XV.2 (1963), 151-157.

Shaull, Richard. "The God-Man Relationship in the Modern World According to Bonhoeffer's Letters." <u>Dimension</u> I.1 (Princeton Theological Seminary).

Soelle, Dorothy. "Who Am I? Dietrich Bonhoeffer?" in <u>Death by Bread Alone</u>, 111-118. Philadelphia: Fortress, 1978.

Smith, Ronald Gregor. "A Theological Perspective on the Secular." <u>The Christian Scholar</u> XLIII.1 (March, 1960), 21ff.

_____, ed. <u>World Come of Age</u>. Philadelphia: Fortress, 1967.

Torrance, T.F. "Bonhoeffer - Myth or Man of Destiny?" The Scotsman (May 28, 1966), 3.

Van Buren, Paul M. "Bonhoeffer's Paradox: Living With God Without God." Union Seminary Quarterly Review XXIII.1 (Fall, 1967), 45-59.

_____. The Secular Meaning of the Gospel. New York: Macmillan, 1963.

Vidler, Alec. "Holy Worldliness." In his Essays in Liberality, 95-112. London: SCM, 1957.

Vorkink, Peter, II, ed. Bonhoeffer in A World Come of Age. Philadelphia: Fortress, 1968.

West, Peggy Joy. Camus and Bonhoeffer. A Comparison of Their Relational Ethic for a Secular World. Ph.D. dissertation, unpublished; University of Arkansas, 1974.

Wiltshire, Susan ford. "Dietrich Bonhoeffer's Prison Poetry." Religion in Life XXXVIII.4 (Winter, 1969), 522-534.

Woelfel, James W. "Bonhoeffer's Portrait of the Religionless Christian." Encounter 28 (Autumn, 1967), 340-367.

Zimmermann, Wolf-Dieter and Ronald Gregor Smith, eds. I Knew Dietrich Bonhoeffer. Reminiscences by his Friends. Translated by Kathe Gregor Smith, New York: Harper, 1966.